THE ART OF PLAYING

THE ART OF PLAYING DEFENSE

HOW TO GET AHEAD BY NOT FALLING BEHIND

WHITNEY TILSON

LIONCREST
PUBLISHING

THE ART OF PLAYING DEFENSE
How to Get Ahead by Not Falling Behind

ISBN 978-1-5445-2032-2 *Hardcover*
      978-1-5445-2031-5 *Paperback*
      978-1-5445-2030-8 *Ebook*
      978-1-5445-2033-9 *Audiobook*

This book is dedicated to my three wonderful daughters, Alison, Emily, and Katharine, who make me proud every day.

If they find even a few nuggets here that help them discover what they want to do with their lives; overcome challenges; avoid setbacks; recover from adversity; seize opportunities; develop deep, loving relationships; achieve genuine happiness; and become the best people they can be, then, to me, the huge effort of writing this book will have been worth it.

And if it's helpful to others as well, that's icing on the cake!

CONTENTS

INTRODUCTION

After nearly two decades of managing money, I closed my hedge funds in September 2017 and launched an educational seminar business through which I sought to teach the next generation of investors everything I'd learned from my time "in the trenches."

My first seminar, with a dozen young investors, was in December 2017. Half of my students were fund managers, while the other half planned to launch funds in the not-too-distant future. Based on their feedback, I developed a curriculum for our five days together that was focused 60% on becoming better investors and 40% on launching and building successful investment-management businesses.

Yet, much to my surprise, over the course of the week, we

ended up spending only about a third of our time on investing and another third on launching a fund.

What was the final third?

Life lessons.

It wasn't my plan to talk about these things, but whenever one of these topics came up, my students would pepper me with questions.

For example, at one point, I mentioned that many of my friends had gotten divorced in recent years. They asked me whether there were any common threads, which eventually led me to develop a list of twelve questions I think anyone should ask before marrying someone.

Another time, one of my students asked how I'd cultivated so many mentors.

"Actually," I replied, "there's a five-step process…" And another long conversation ensued.

It soon dawned on me that teaching them this "worldly wisdom" was just as important as the formal curriculum I'd developed—and could be the basis for a book.

THE FOCUS ON CALAMITIES

When I dove into this book, I started by writing about positive life lessons: work hard, become a learning machine, be nice, have high integrity, etc.

But a few chapters in, I ran out of gas and didn't write a word for months. I'd lost motivation and couldn't figure out why. I finally realized it was because I was having trouble finding anything fresh and interesting to say. How many books are there that extol the virtues of things like hard work and developing good habits? Thousands! Sure, this stuff is important, but it's all been said and written a million times before, so I didn't feel like I was adding much.

But the calamities section I'd planned for the end of the book—now *that* was interesting! How many books are there about all of the horrible things that can ruin your life like cancer, a terrible accident, your marriage falling apart, getting thrown in jail, losing all your money, having no friends, or becoming addicted to drugs or alcohol?

I'd developed a slide presentation on calamities and, each time I taught it, my audience was riveted!

So I decided to change the focus—and title—of this book.

Fair warning: much of this book is a downer. Who likes to think about all the bad things that can derail your life? Most people would rather think optimistically and hope for the best. But if you don't also think about avoiding calamities, you're making a big mistake.

The foundation for a successful life is playing good defense. If you want to get ahead, it's critical to avoid big setbacks.

WHY ME?

At first glance, I may seem like the wrong person to be writing a book about calamities because I've suffered few of them.

I grew up all over the world in a loving, tight-knit family, I earned degrees from Harvard and Harvard Business School, I've been a (mostly) successful serial entrepreneur, my wife Susan and I are still happily married after 27 years and have three spectacular daughters, I'm in great health, and I have many wonderful friends. You can see why I count my blessings every day...

So why am I qualified to write this book?

Let me answer that question by asking one: If you wanted to learn to play tennis better, would you hire me or Roger Federer? For basketball, me or Steph Curry?

Similarly, if you want to learn how to avoid calamities,

would you rather learn from someone who's suffered a lot of them or someone who's successfully avoided them?

It's not an accident that I've suffered far fewer than my fair share of big setbacks. Rather, it's primarily the result of two things. During my youth, I had two wonderful role models—my parents—both of whom I love and admire more than anyone. They surrounded me with love from the day I was born and made big sacrifices for my sister Dana and me.

By being excellent teachers and role models, they helped me avoid the calamities of youth: I didn't get myself killed, stayed away from drugs and alcohol, and got a great education.

Then, as an adult, in addition to having a wonderful wife, I've had two more wonderful role models: famed investors Warren Buffett and Charlie Munger.

When I discovered them in the mid-1990s as I was first getting interested in investing, I studied them obsessively, reading everything by and about them and traveling to Omaha to attend the Berkshire Hathaway annual meeting every May (I'd been to 21 in a row until the coronavirus forced the cancellation of the 2020 meeting).

What I learned from these two wise men about investing was invaluable. In the early days of my career, I had so little experience—and they were such brilliant, inspiring, and patient teachers! Had I not absorbed all of the investing lessons they imparted, I would never have achieved anything close to what I did. I beat the market year after year in my first dozen years and grew assets under management from $1 million to $200 million across three hedge funds and two mutual funds. I also launched successful investment conference and newsletter businesses, appeared regularly on CNBC for many years, was on *60 Minutes* twice, wrote hundreds of articles, and coauthored three books.

I've come to realize, though, that the most important things I learned (and continue to learn) from Buffett and Munger go well beyond value investing. They fall under the category of what Munger calls "worldly wisdom."

Much of what they preach is simple (as Munger jokes, "If it's trite, it's right!"): work hard, become a learning machine, have high integrity, develop good habits, be nice to everyone, marry the right person and maintain a strong relationship, and so forth.

They also spend a lot of time talking about calamities. I still remember the moment when I was at the WESCO annual meeting two decades ago when Munger said, "All I want to know is where I'm going to die, so I never go there."

Everybody laughed, but he continued:

"I'm serious. Once you reach a certain position in life, you should spend most of your time trying to avoid the things that can derail your life and send you back to "go," or worse. That's true in investing, but it's also true in life. What happens to many people is that even when they've got it made, they can't help but stretch to try to grab the brass ring—and fall, bringing themselves to ruin."

Ever since, I've been studying calamities. Avoiding calamities is all about assessing risk—and that's what I've been doing full-time for more than two decades in the investment world. Most people aren't very good at it because they tend to focus on vivid but unlikely risks while ignoring far more dangerous ones right in front of them.

For example, when I started mountaineering a few years ago, summiting hairy peaks like the Matterhorn and the Eiger, my mom flipped out. She begged me to stop and, when I refused, tried to enlist Susan in an "intervention."

I explained to her that she was worried about the wrong thing. I'd estimate that I'm *ten times* more likely to die riding my bicycle nearly every day on the streets of Manhattan than climbing mountains a few days a year.

Another risk many people ignore until it's too late is the risk of their marriage going bad. In recent years, I've seen this derail the lives of over a dozen close friends and relatives.

In each case, I asked them to tell me what happened so I could learn from it and take steps to ensure it didn't happen to Susan and me.

A final example I'll cite is car safety. In the past two years, my wife, three cousins, and three friends have been in seven—SEVEN!—serious accidents. In each case, their cars were totaled, resulting in multiple concussions and, tragically, two deaths. This affected me deeply and, even though our 10-year-old Volvo was running fine and built like a tank, led me to buy a new car—the exact same model, but with a lot more safety features. It was a wise decision, as Susan was in a serious accident not long afterward.

CALAMITY #1

LOSS OF REPUTATION AND/OR WEALTH

If you're in the professional world—if you are, for example, a doctor, lawyer, or businessperson—your greatest asset other than your brain is your reputation, for how hard you work, your sense of decency, and most importantly, your integrity.

Cherish and protect it because, as Buffett once said:

> "It takes 20 years to build a reputation and five minutes to ruin it. If you think about that, you'll do things differently.
>
> I want employees to ask themselves whether they are willing to have any contemplated act appear the next day on the front of their local paper, to be read by their spouses, children, and

friends, with the reporting done by an informed and critical reporter."

You need to be especially careful of your reputation if you're a public figure, on whom the scrutiny is greater. I am extremely sensitive to this danger because I send an investing-related email to more than 125,000 people every weekday, an education-related one to 7,500 folks every week or two, a coronavirus-related one to more than 5,000 people every week, and a few every day to 250-1,000 recipients on various subjects, ranging from politics to adventure sports to what my family and I are up to. In addition, I regularly speak on live television, at conferences, and to reporters.

Thus, multiple times a day, I run the risk that I will write or say something off the cuff that goes viral and ruins my reputation. I've made some small mistakes that have really scared me.

Right out of college, as I was helping Wendy Kopp launch Teach for America, I was interviewed by a reporter for the *Harvard Crimson*. In making a point about teacher shortages in low-income communities, I said, "Many school districts just need warm bodies."

This crude and foolish comment was, of course, featured prominently in the article.

Wendy was so mad at me—deservedly so—that she never let me speak to the media again.

Years later, I sent an email to my school-reform email list in which I commented on the then-Mayor of Newark, New Jersey, Sharpe James, who was facing corruption charges. Being certain of his guilt (he was later convicted and served time in prison), I sent around an article about his indictment with the comment, "Hang him high!"

A few minutes later, someone emailed me back saying, "Whitney, did you really mean to use language related to lynching when referring to a black man?"

Of course not! I was horrified by what I'd written and immediately sent an apologetic follow-up email.

Another time, I was on Bloomberg TV talking about Taser, a stock I was betting against (it's since been renamed Axon). In explaining why I said that the company had no patents or valuable intellectual property.

About a week later, I received an email from Taser's law firm saying I had defamed the company because it did, in fact, hold numerous patents and demanded a retraction.

I had screwed up again. By not being careful with my words, I had exposed myself to substantial legal costs at the very least.

Fortunately, I was able to resolve the issue by replying with a letter apologizing for my mistake, pledging never to speak publicly about the stock again, and pointing out that if they forced me to publicly issue a retraction, it would only draw attention to an otherwise obscure interview that almost no one had seen. I never heard from them again, so it ended up being a low-cost lesson early in my career to be very careful when publicly criticizing a company.

Almost every day, I see a public figure in trouble for something they said or wrote (usually an off-the-cuff remark).

I don't want this to happen to me, so now I proofread every mass email before I send it and always try to be well-prepared when I speak on television, in front of an audience, or to a reporter.

Another way to ruin your reputation is to do something unethical or illegal (which can lead to a loss of freedom—i.e., going to prison).

Consider the fate of David Sokol, a former top executive at Berkshire Hathaway who was once rumored to be Buffett's successor. He discovered a publicly traded chemical company called Lubrizol that he thought would be a great acquisition candidate for Berkshire Hathaway, so he brought this idea to Buffett, who agreed and eventually acquired the company.

However, inexplicably, Sokol had personally bought Lubrizol stock beforehand, thereby profiting from Berkshire Hathaway's acquisition. As soon as Buffett found out what Sokol had done, he had no choice but to immediately fire him and report what had happened to the US Securities and Exchange Commission (SEC). The SEC ultimately took no action, but it didn't matter—Sokol's reputation was destroyed, and his career was over, all for an insignificant profit. For a single moment, he let greed overshadow his integrity, and he was ruined.

It's critical to be disciplined and thoughtful about ethical gray areas and never engage in borderline (much less illegal) behavior. It's simple in concept but can be tricky in practice, and there's no room for error. One mistake can ruin your life.

Over the nearly two decades that I ran a hedge fund, there were so many opportunities to break the law and/or ruin my reputation. Most of these situations were pretty clear, but some weren't.

For example, what if I talk to the CEO of a small company, and I suspect (but am not sure) he might have given me material nonpublic information? Or if I talk to a reporter who I think (but am not sure) is writing an article that might cause a stock to move sharply? Or if I'm preparing an in-depth presentation of a stock idea at a major conference that I think (but am not sure) could move the stock materially?

Can I trade these stocks? To this day, I don't know the answer. So I just didn't.

Here's an example related to the stock for which I'm perhaps best known, Lumber Liquidators. I bet against the stock and pitched it at the Robin Hood Investors Conference in late 2013. Then, in early 2014, I heard from someone in the industry that the company was sourcing and selling Chinese-made laminate flooring tainted with formaldehyde, a health hazard and clear violation of US environmental regulations. Once I'd tested the product and verified my source's story, I wanted to bring attention to what this company was doing, both to protect American consumers and because I thought it might crush the stock (and therefore benefit my short position).

"Who better," I thought, "than *60 Minutes* to break this story?" So I contacted a producer I knew there and, to make a long story short, they agreed it was an important story and started working on it.

At that point, I didn't know for sure if *60 Minutes* was going to run the story, what it would say, or when it might air. But by December 2014, when Anderson Cooper interviewed me at length, I was pretty sure that they were going to do a major story that could devastate the stock (which is exactly what happened in March 2015), so I could have made millions of dollars had I further increased my short position.

But I didn't. I worried that the knowledge I had about *60 Minutes* working on the story constituted inside information. To this day, I'm not sure if it did, but I didn't want to find out the hard way, and, to me, it didn't pass the front-page-of-the-newspaper test. So I didn't trade the stock at all until after the story aired.

I can't emphasize strongly enough that no amount of money is worth jeopardizing your reputation.

YOUR WORST 1%

It's important to understand that you aren't judged for the way you behave 90% or even 95% of the time, but rather on your worst 1%—or even 0.01%.

To my knowledge, David Sokol had never done anything unethical in his long career before his fateful purchase of Lubrizol's stock ruined him. That's all it took.

In my two decades as a hedge fund manager, I made thousands of trades. To my knowledge, all were ethical and proper, but if even one hadn't been, I could have been ruined as well.

One misjudgment is all it takes, so avoid gray areas. Never go near the line. Be ultraconservative when it comes to your integrity and reputation.

This applies to every area of life. You can be a kind and generous person almost all of the time, but if you make one blatantly racist or sexist remark (even if you're not racist or sexist), that's what you will be remembered for.

Even if you've been faithful to your spouse for decades, if you go to Vegas one weekend, get drunk, and have a one-night stand, you've likely permanently ruined your marriage.

The implications of the worst-one-percent reality are sobering. Everyone makes mistakes, but in some areas, you simply can't afford to make any.

There are many things you can do to avoid this kind of calamity. First, mistakes are far more likely if you're sleep-deprived or under physical, mental, or financial duress, so, if at all possible, avoid taking important actions or making big decisions under these conditions.

Be careful who you associate with, both personally and professionally. Their behavior and reputation will rub off on you and vice versa.

And never assume that something is private or off the

record. Other than perhaps the most intimate conversations with your closest friends and family, assume that everything you write and say is being recorded and could be made public. Emails, in particular, live forever, so it's best to assume that someday they will be read by a hostile journalist, regulator, investigator, or lawyer. It's happened to me a few times, and it's no fun.

LOSS OF WEALTH

I'll acknowledge that the calamity of losing your wealth is a high-class problem (it can only happen to people who have money!).

If you're fortunate enough to have a comfortable income and healthy savings, it might be nice to think about making even more, but it's far more important to make sure you don't lose what you already have.

Ironically, the surest, fastest way to get poor quickly is to try to get rich quickly. I've known people who spent their whole lives building up their savings only to lose it all in some crazy, half-baked scheme. Common examples include investing everything in their own new business—or someone else's—and it fails; speculating in penny stocks; day trading stocks or, worse yet, options; or getting duped by some online or phone fraudster. Millions of people are ensnared in these traps every year.

Another way to become poor, albeit somewhat more slowly, is to lose a good job and not be able to replace it. Or get divorced—boom, there goes half your wealth, plus expenses usually rise (two homes, less favorable tax treatment, etc.).

But the most common way to get into financial trouble is to spend more than you earn (after taxes). What this means is that every year, you need to borrow money to fill the gap—and there are lenders galore who will sell you—at a steep price—all the rope you need to hang yourself: credit card companies, installment lenders, auto dealers, and so forth.

To be clear, certain types of debt are fine. It often makes sense to take out a subsidized student loan for a high-quality education or to buy a reasonably valued house with a fixed-rate, low-interest, tax-deductible mortgage. But otherwise, it's usually best to avoid debt.

Our economy and, in particular, our financial system is, in many ways, incredibly predatory. It makes it so easy to spend, luring people into living above their means. It is imperative that you resist this siren song. No matter what your income, figure out a way to live within it.

DEVELOP GOOD FINANCIAL HABITS

If you want to build wealth and live comfortably someday, you need to develop good financial habits. A 1996 book called *The Millionaire Next Door* shaped my thinking on this topic. The authors refuted many misconceptions about financial success, chiefly the idea that to become wealthy, you have to inherit money or have a high-paying job like a Wall Street banker, celebrity, or professional athlete.

Instead, the authors discovered that the most common job among millionaires was running a small, private business. The second most common was a professional like a doctor or teacher.

But, in a fascinating finding, it turned out that income level was only moderately predictive of whether someone would become a millionaire. More important was whether someone *lived beneath their means*, year in and year out. In their survey of millionaires, the factor that most closely correlated to whether someone was a millionaire was whether they answered "yes" to the question: "Is your spouse more frugal than you are?"

Doctors, on average, earn quite a bit more than teachers. Yet, relative to their income, they are less likely to become millionaires because they tend to spend all—or more than all—of their high incomes on big houses in upscale neighborhoods, new cars, country club memberships, fancy vacations, private schools, and so forth.

Meanwhile, teachers are far more likely to become millionaires than their incomes would predict because they tend to live frugally.

My parents, both teachers, are perfect examples. They can squeeze a dollar until it screams. Growing up, we almost never went out to eat—going to Friendly's once a month was such a treat! My mom clipped dozens of coupons from the circular in the Sunday paper and, when she came home from the supermarket, would crow about how much she'd saved. And she bought most of our clothes at second-hand stores. She still tells my sister and me that our costly educations were funded by her thriftiness.

We never had a new car. My dad is a good mechanic, so we always bought 10-year-old cars that he would nurse along for years. I remember in the 1980s when we lived in western Massachusetts, we had a beaten-up 1960s vintage Mercedes. Its heater had stopped working long ago, which was a big problem during the bitterly cold winters. But no matter—we all bundled up in our down jackets and used de-icer spray on the inside of the windows.

Similarly, Buffett, despite being one of the wealthiest men in the world, is still very frugal. He could afford to live in a massive estate, but instead has lived in the same house for 61 years! When he first started flying in a private jet, he felt so embarrassed that he nicknamed it "The Indefensible."

SAVE AND INVEST

Once you've developed good financial habits and are saving money every year, you need to invest your savings wisely.

The good news is that it's not hard.

First, max out your retirement plan(s) like an IRA or 401k—especially if your employer will match at least some portion of it (this is free money—take it!). Tax-deferred savings are much more valuable than taxable ones because you won't have to pay taxes on your realized gains each year. The difference over time is enormous. Also, because there's a penalty for taking the money out before you're 65 years old, you're less likely to do something stupid with it.

Ideally, set up automatic withholding from your paycheck into your IRA (or another retirement fund)—this makes it easier to save because you never see the money.

Then, set up a plan such that the moment the money hits your account, it's automatically invested in an S&P 500 index fund. (If you want to set aside some money to invest on your own, that's fine—sign up for my newsletters at Empire Financial Research to help you do so—but index most of it.)

Finally—this is key—don't look at it! Just let it build, year after year, decade after decade. Whatever you do, don't panic during times of market turmoil and sell—just about everybody who does this has terrible timing, selling at exactly the wrong time (for example, in March 2009 or 2020).

Consider the extreme case of my sister, who had a retirement account at her old employer, then switched jobs—and *forgot about it*! Years later, she remembered it—and discovered *hundreds of thousands of dollars* (!) because she'd done everything right up front: her employer automatically withdrew the maximum retirement contribution from her paycheck and then invested all of it in an S&P 500 index fund.

When my parents moved to Africa 24 years ago, first to Ethiopia and then, nine years later, to Kenya, where they've since retired, I took charge of their financial affairs. Though neither of them had ever had a big salary, they had both worked for their entire careers, earned decent incomes, and lived super frugally. As a result, they had built up a nest egg of around $800,000.

But they were much too conservative in how they'd invested it. Though they were still in their mid-fifties and would likely work another 15 years and live into their nineties, their savings were mostly in cash and bonds—an allocation more appropriate for eighty-year-olds.

So I put a third of their savings into my hedge fund and

another third into an index fund, such that two-thirds of their savings were in stocks.

It was the right call. Two decades later, they're in their late-seventies, and their net worth is multiples of what it once was. They're comfortably retired—though you wouldn't know it from how frugal they still are. When they came back to the US for a couple of months last summer, as they do every year, my mom refused to get a SIM card for her Kenya cell phone that would allow her to make and receive calls, get her email, etc. because it cost too much: one dollar per day!

CALAMITY #2

═══

LONELINESS AND/OR SUFFERING A PERMANENTLY IMPAIRED RELATIONSHIP WITH A LOVED ONE

Imagine a condition that makes a person irritable, depressed, and self-centered and is associated with a 26% increase in the risk of premature mortality. Imagine too that in industrialised countries, around a third of people are affected by this condition, with one person in 12 affected severely, and that these proportions are increasing. Income, education, sex, and ethnicity are not protective, and the condition is contagious. The effects of the condition are not attributable to some peculiarity of the character of a subset of individuals; they are a result of the condition affecting ordinary people. Such a condition exists—loneliness.

—THE GROWING PROBLEM OF LONELINESS, PUBLISHED IN *THE LANCET* IN 2018

There are few things more important than having strong relationships.

Since 1938, researchers have been following 268 Harvard College sophomores in one of the world's longest studies of adult life called the *Harvard Study of Adult Development* (only 19 were still alive as of April 2017). An article in the *Harvard Gazette* about the study noted:

> Over the years, researchers have studied the participants' health trajectories and their broader lives, including their triumphs and failures in careers and marriage, and the findings have produced startling lessons, and not only for the researchers.

> "The surprising finding is that our relationships and how happy we are in our relationships has a powerful influence on our health," said Robert Waldinger, director of the study, a Psychiatrist at Massachusetts General Hospital, and a Professor of Psychiatry at Harvard Medical School. "Taking care of your body is important, but tending to your relationships is a form of self-care too. That, I think, is the revelation."

Close relationships, more than money or fame, are what keep people happy throughout their lives. Those ties protect people from life's discontents, delay mental and physical decline, and are better predictors of long and happy lives than social class, IQ, or even genes.

"When we gathered together everything we knew about them at age 50, it wasn't their middle-aged cholesterol levels that predicted how they were going to grow old," said Waldinger in a popular TED Talk. "It was how satisfied they were in their relationships. The people who were the most satisfied in their relationships at age 50 were the healthiest at age 80."

You might think that close relationships would be flourishing in today's hyperconnected world of free or low-cost phone/video calls, email, texting, and connections with endless numbers of people via Facebook, Instagram, Snapchat, etc.

Yet, the opposite is occurring. Even before the coronavirus, which has surely made things much worse, the US had been experiencing a loneliness epidemic. A 2018 study from health insurer Cigna found that 54% of 20,000 Americans surveyed reported feeling lonely—and this rose to 61% only a year later. According to other studies, two in five Americans report they sometimes or always feel their social interactions lack meaning, and one in five reports chronic loneliness or social isolation. More than half of American adults are unmarried, and a quarter live alone.

It cuts across all age groups. The American Association of Retired Persons (AARP) reports that more than 42 million adults in the US over the age of 45 suffer from chronic loneliness and that loneliness and isolation are major risk factors for early death in older Americans, increasing the odds by 45%. Meanwhile, the Cigna study found that Generation Z adults (18-22 years old) are the loneliest generation, outpacing boomers, Gen X, and millennials, despite being more connected than ever.

While it may seem counterintuitive, it turns out that social media is causing loneliness and misery for two primary reasons: first, people are substituting social media for genuine in-person interactions, and second, because they only see other people's "highlight reels" (cherry-picked photos of seemingly perfect trips, parties, and relationships), they assume that everyone else's lives are better than their own.

We are just beginning to understand the many negative effects of chronic loneliness. Researchers at the Health Resources and Services Administration found social isolation is as damaging to human health as smoking fifteen cigarettes a day and more dangerous than obesity. Conversely, greater social connection is associated with a 50% reduced risk of early death.

Why does loneliness cause poor health? It turns out that it compromises immune responses, increases the production of stress hormones, and disrupts sleep. These issues can lead to chronic inflammation, which lowers immunity, ages the body, and increases the risk of heart disease, Type 2 diabetes, arthritis, and cognitive decline. Socially isolated adults are twice as likely to develop Alzheimer's disease, 32% more likely to have a stroke, and 29% more likely to experience coronary heart disease. The chronically lonely are even more susceptible to the common cold!

Loneliness is also dangerous because people living alone (especially the elderly and disabled) are less likely to see a doctor when needed, take medications, exercise, and monitor their diets.

COMBATTING LONELINESS

To combat loneliness, you first have to overcome the natural inclination to withdraw even further. An 11-year study by psychologists at the University of Chicago revealed that many lonely people feel under threat and, to protect themselves, respond by becoming more self-centered, which of course, just makes them lonelier still.

The key is to overcome these fears and invest in building more, deeper relationships. Both breadth and depth are important, though I think the latter is more so.

What's a deep friendship? I've always thought that this was a good test: would they hide you? During the Holocaust, when the Nazis murdered more than six million Jews in Europe, some survived because their non-Jewish friends hid them—risking their own lives to do so. This is how Anne Frank and her family survived for more than two years in Amsterdam before they were betrayed.

Building deep relationships like this requires effort. It starts by meeting people, perhaps at work or at shared-interest organizations where there are likely to be people with values and interests similar to yours (religion, hobbies, volunteering, dog-walking, a book club, etc.). Get out of the house and don't be shy; a stranger is only a stranger until you get to know them.

Then, once you've met someone, look for ways to build and deepen the relationship. If you read an article or come across a website that you think would interest them, send a quick email. I do this dozens of times a day on an individual level and have also put together two dozen email lists on topics such as particular stocks, investing, school reform, politics, Africa, and adventure sports. It's a quick and efficient method of regularly touching dozens, hundreds, even thousands of people in a positive way.

That said, don't confuse mass emails or posting on social media with real relationship building. For that, look for any excuse to call or meet someone. A phone call is far more personal than an email, and an in-person meeting is best of all. Invite them for a coffee, a meal, or a movie, or go to a museum (if they ever reopen!). Put everyone's birthday in your calendar and send them a personal note on their special day. I do this for more than 500 people—and always include lots of pictures from the good times we've had together.

And of course, always be responsive—reply to emails and texts, enthusiastically greet anyone who calls, and say yes if someone invites you to something. There's an old—and true—saying that "80% of life is just showing up."

CHOOSING FRIENDS

It's wonderful to have lots of casual friends but choose your close ones carefully. Good ones will enrich your life immensely, while bad ones will drag you down—not only directly but also because others will judge you based on them.

Buffett once said:

> "You will move in the direction of the people you associate with, so it's important to associate with people better than yourself. You want to associate yourself with people who are the kind of person that you'd like to be. You'll move in

that direction. The friends you have will form you as you go through life. Make some good friends and keep them for the rest of your life. Have them be people you admire as well as like."

I tend to like everyone initially. Susan says it's my worst—but also my best—trait. Sometimes, it results in less-than-ideal people entering my orbit, but I'm getting better about recognizing them and quietly disengaging without burning bridges or creating enemies.

Here are some questions to ask when deciding on whether to invest in a deep friendship with someone:

1. Are they kind and good-hearted toward you and others?
2. Do they have high integrity? Do you trust them?
3. Are they stable, solid, and predictable?
4. Do you share core values?
5. Are they intelligent and intellectually curious? Do you find them interesting?
6. Do they like to do fun things and have a zest for life?

IMPAIRED RELATIONSHIPS WITH LOVED ONES

A separate but related calamity to loneliness is a permanently impaired relationship with a loved one—in particular, a parent, sibling, or child. It can be as devastating as a divorce (I cover spousal relationships in a later chapter).

As Buffett once said, "I know of so many people with all the money in the world, but they're divorced, don't talk to their kids, and are totally miserable. *My definition of success is whether the people who should love you do love you.*"

My grandfather didn't speak to his brother for the last forty years of their lives due to some silly argument. Both were too stubborn to reach out and bury the hatchet. How stupid and unnecessary!

There are two keys to avoiding this calamity: maintain healthy relationships in your family and, if a relationship breaks, fix it!

The quiet disengagement I recommended for people you want to unfriend doesn't really work when it comes to family. I don't know anyone who is truly fond of every single person in their extended family (including their spouse's family), which presents a dilemma: to some extent, you can minimize the time you spend with the family member(s) you don't care for, but at the end of the day, you're stuck with them.

You can, however, choose how you behave toward them. If you're foolish, you'll wear your feelings on your sleeve and let them know that you don't like them very much. You'll ignore them, or, worse yet, be snitty and unpleasant. And, of course, they'll respond in kind.

Or, you can be pragmatic, wise, and mature. If you're going to have to be around them for the rest of your life, why not try to at least have a civil relationship—and, ideally, a friendly one? Make an effort to talk to and show genuine interest in them. It's not so hard. And who knows? Maybe you'll end up liking them!

If you do have a blowout with a loved one, it's often not too difficult to fix if you're smart and proactive.

I've been friends with Senator Cory Booker for more than two decades and think the world of him, so last fall, I sent an email to my friends and family asking them to support his run for president. Dozens did so, but one of my cousins wrote back saying, "Seriously, you are so much smarter than that!" and then added some nasty things about Cory, including calling him a racist (seriously).

I should have just ignored her reply, but I didn't. I thought her email was ignorant and obnoxious, plus I had just flown to Europe and was sleep-deprived, jet-lagged, and crabby.

So I blasted her...and she blasted me back...and a thermonuclear war of emails ensued!

It caused a knot in my stomach. While I felt like I was in the right—and she had started the argument—I also had a sinking feeling that this could impair our half-century-long relationship.

I was still stewing over this the next day when I decided to pick up the phone and call her. To break the tension, I opened with the line, "Hey, it's your favorite cousin calling!"

She burst out laughing, we had a good talk about our pissing contest, and we quickly buried the hatchet.

There are some good lessons here:

1. Don't talk politics with anyone you know who strongly disagrees with you. In today's polarized world, politics is like religion. Can you imagine two people from different religions having a discussion, with each trying to persuade the other that their religion is inferior and that they should switch? No good can come of it—only anger, hurt feelings, and a ruptured relationship. No wonder one-third of Americans say that political disagreements have resulted in one or more impaired relationships.
2. If you get angry with someone, wait a day before replying so you have a chance to cool off. As Munger likes to say: "You can always tell someone to go to hell tomorrow."
3. Email and texting are great for efficiently communicating information but are horrible for anything delicate or

emotional. In these cases, communicate in person or, if that's not possible, pick up the phone and call.

4. If you screw up 1, 2, and 3, as I did, it's usually still not too late to go see someone in person or call them and try to make things right. It's very easy to be a total jerk in a text or email, but much harder in person.

LITTLE WAYS I TRY TO BUILD RELATIONSHIPS

There are a million little ways you can make a difference in others' lives. Here are some I try to do regularly:

- I try to remember, acknowledge, and celebrate others' special events: birthdays, weddings, anniversaries, births of children, etc.
- Whenever I learn someone's birthday, I put a reminder in my calendar on that date to send them a happy birthday email. And not only that, I create a folder on my hard drive with photos of them so I can include fun pictures as well. I now have 497 birthdays in my calendar, and those 497 folders contain nearly 25,000 pictures.
- When I go to a major event like a friend's wedding or birthday party, I usually bring my camera and take a lot of pictures. When I get home, I pick the best ones, send them to my friend, and (with their permission) post them on social media. Sometimes, I even make a photo album to surprise them. I've done this at a number of friends' weddings—it's a unique and special gift that

they always cherish. The two or three hours it takes me to make an album is time well spent.

- Anytime my wife and I learn that a friend, or even an acquaintance, has had a baby, we send a baby gift.
- If a friend is being honored at a charity event, I show up. If they ask me to support a charity, I make a donation—even small donations earn so much goodwill.
- Anytime I read an article that I think would be of interest to someone, I send it to them. I do this more than a dozen times every day.
- On an almost daily basis, someone interested in investing emails me a question or asks for help finding a job. I always try to reply and be helpful. I get job requests so often I published an article more than a dozen years ago entitled "Breaking into Money Management," so I always have something to send to job seekers.
- If I find a mess, I usually clean it up—even if I didn't make it. If I find dirty dishes in the sink, I either wash them or put them in the dishwasher. When I'm walking around my neighborhood, I pick up trash pretty much every day—and when I'm out walking my dog, that means other dogs' poop! Yes, it's gross, but it's even more gross to leave it there for someone to step in.

I could go on, but you get the idea. I try to go through life deliberately, consciously, and energetically looking for opportunities to do something nice for someone else, even if it's something really small. (My favorite book about this is *Give and Take: Why Helping Others Drives Our Success* by Adam Grant.)

RELATIONSHIP WITH YOUR CHILDREN

Having a strong, loving relationship with my children is incredibly important to me. Even though I'm sometimes preoccupied and overworked, I hope my daughters know that I love them unconditionally and will always be there for them.

I take pride in being an uncool father in terms of curfews, drinking, dating, talking back, appropriate dress, getting cell phones, watching TV, and so forth.

Bad parenting drives me crazy. I see a lot of kids, even very young ones, doing pretty much whatever they want and walking all over their parents.

This is one of my hot buttons. I just won't tolerate it. I think it's important for children to have boundaries—and if I occasionally have to get angry to enforce those boundaries, so be it.

At one point, when my older daughters were much younger and were constantly fighting and misbehaving, I lost my cool so often that they told me they thought I had an anger management problem.

I, of course, lost my cool yet again and yelled at them: "Have you ever once seen me get angry at anybody else except you guys?!"

They had to admit that they hadn't, so I continued:

"The problem here isn't *my* anger management, but *your* behavior! Behave yourselves and don't be rude and disrespectful, and I'll stop getting angry with you!"

Believe it or not, that was actually a turning point for all of us. We'd gotten into bad habits, but once we cleared the air and made an effort, things improved.

I want my children to respect me and view me as an honest truth-teller. They all played multiple varsity sports in high school, and if they had a bad game, I didn't tell them how great they played. Instead, I'd say something like, "That was a tough game. Keep practicing, and you'll do better next time."

HOW TO CULTIVATE MENTORS AND DEVELOP DEEP RELATIONSHIPS

Once while I was teaching a seminar, a student—a young man in his twenties—wrote me the following email:

When I launched my fund, I found myself in a position with

no mentors. I didn't have a boss anymore to give me feedback and mentor me so that I would perform better.

I have made lots of connections among peers (people who launched their funds over the past few years), but it is a different type of relationship—mainly discussing ideas.

So I have always been thinking: 'How can I find a mentor in the space?' Even when I found more experienced fund managers (let's say 10 years ahead of me) and I was able to get their attention because of my research, it was difficult to move that relationship beyond discussing ideas ('Hey, here is a great one! You should look into it', 'Thank you! Here is one from me!').

I totally get it—people are very, very busy. However, if I can be better at building that relationship, it can move the needle.

In response, I put together a teaching module that, while specific to cultivating mentors, can be applied more broadly to building, maintaining, and deepening all types of relationships.

I started by outlining the five steps to cultivating mentors:

1. Pick a target
2. Pre-contact preparation
3. Initial contact

4. Follow-ups
5. Long-term relationship building

Below, I'll share that teaching module and, throughout, also detail how to adapt each of the five points for use toward building personal relationships.

PICK A TARGET

Before you can cultivate a mentor (or develop a friendship), you first have to pick a target—who do you want to be your mentor or friend? A mentor is an experienced and trusted advisor who can help you in your life and career (and ideally become a great friend).

Typical candidates might be your boss (or someone else at work, ideally very senior), someone who can help you build your business (investor or board member), a professor/teacher, a sports coach, or simply someone you admire and would like to learn from and befriend.

Be realistic, however. Neither the Pope nor Barack Obama is likely to become your mentor. That said, sometimes aiming high pays off (for me, Buffett and Munger).

PRE-CONTACT PREPARATION

People *really* like it when others show a genuine interest

in them. So if you want someone to become a mentor (or just a new friend), you must show genuine interest in and appreciation for them.

To do so, in the case of a mentor, you need to know as much as possible about them. So, before contacting them, start with a Google search so you can demonstrate that you do your homework. Show your interest in them, and learn about connections (college, kids, pets, sports, travel, language, culture, etc.) that, over time, can lead to good feelings, bonding, and mentorship. Ditto if you've just met someone you think you'd like to be friends with.

Then look for other ways to gain insight. For example, when I learned that Anderson Cooper would be interviewing me about Lumber Liquidators on *60 Minutes*, I read his autobiography and discovered many connections. For instance, he was a Yale '89 political science major who traveled around Africa after graduating, while I'm a Harvard '89 political science major who's lived and traveled extensively in Africa.

Knowing a lot about someone will allow you to find multiple ways to engage with them and build a relationship.

INITIAL CONTACT

Be succinct—the initial contact is usually a conversation lasting less than a minute or an email no longer than two to three paragraphs. Your goal is to make a good first impression so that when you follow up (of course, get their card), they'll remember you and be inclined to agree to a meeting, take your call, or respond to your email.

Flatter them—who doesn't love this?—but it must be genuine. Don't be obsequious. If there's an opportunity, ask thoughtful questions and get them talking.

Don't appear nervous (even if you are)—you must project an air of confidence that you are an interesting person who is going to be valuable to them in many, many ways over time (and then, of course, deliver on this promise!).

See if you can figure out a way that you can add value to them (e.g., offer to send them information about a stock they own or a great new stock idea you have that's likely to be in their sweet spot—if not during the initial contact, then soon after).

TIPS TO GETTING THROUGH TO A BUSY PERSON

If you have any connection at all, use it. Try to meet in person—go to an event where you know they'll be, such as a conference or charity event. Set up a Google alert to stay abreast of where they might be speaking.

If that's not possible, send an email (I generally advise not calling unless you've been introduced to the person and they're expecting it).

Prepare to be persistent—but no stalking!—and don't get discouraged by rejection. The job of an assistant is to make you go away—don't take it personally. Find out the assistant's name and be polite and gracious to them. They're the gateway to your potential mentor.

Don't remind your potential mentor or their assistant that you've called or emailed in the past. They probably won't remember, and making them feel guilty is unlikely to help you.

Once you get a response, follow up quickly.

EXAMPLES OF COMPELLING INITIAL CONTACTS

Here's a great example of an email a young guy sent me five years ago:

> Dear Whitney,
>
> I attended your Value Investing Congress a couple of years ago in NYC. I am running a long/short equity hedge fund with offices in NYC and Tel Aviv, where I am currently based.
>
> I have noticed you've recently opened a long position on

SodaStream. We are about to complete quite a thorough short thesis on the stock, and I was wondering if you would consider exchanging ideas? Being based in Israel, we have good access to the company and have performed thorough due diligence.

Looking forward to hearing from you.

Best regards,

Gabriel

In the first sentence, Gabriel tells me that he's a paying customer of my conference business; in the second, that he's a fellow long/short hedge fund manager. Check, check.

Then he offers to share information about a company whose stock I own. The company is based in Israel, and he has an office there, which gives me reason to believe that his information might be particularly valuable.

Naturally, I responded immediately, and we've since developed a strong professional and personal relationship.

Here's another one—perhaps the best I've ever read:

Dear Mr. Tilson:

We have never met. My name is Angelo Martorell, and I am

a recent 2015 Wharton MBA grad. I am a fan of yours both in the investing world and more recently in regards to your stance regarding our current president. Like him, I went to Wharton; unlike him, I was born in Mexico.

I had an incredibly tough time recruiting for an investment job during and after my MBA. Even though I won more stock pitch competitions than anybody at Wharton, including the Boston Investment Conference and the Sohn Investment competition, employers such as Baupost, Tiger Global, and about 100 other hedge funds found a way to ding me.

After finding a position on a fund that soon after closed shop, I started my own fund with $4 millions. I have a 120% return since June 2016.

I respect your knowledge on investments—sometimes we are on the same side, and sometimes on the opposite. I believe you are a great person of integrity. I am completely self-taught and have sold a business as a CFO before Wharton in CA. I am a 6x cycling national champion in both Mexico and the US.

Bottom line is I have no mentor. I have found few people to trust in this industry. I went through community college when I moved to the US when I was 17, and my family has no connections.

If you have time to chat or feel inclined to give advice, you would have no idea how much it would mean to me.

Very best regards and from a Mexican—Gracias,

Angelo Martorell, CFA, Martorell Capital Partners, LLC

Pretty much every sentence here is compelling and personal—either to him or to me. Angelo had clearly done his homework.

I was happy to meet with Angelo. He became one of my first students at Kase Learning, and as with Gabriel, he and I now also have a close professional and personal relationship.

FOLLOW-UPS

When you follow up on the initial contact, they might not remember you, so remind them who you are and thank them for having taken the time to meet/email you earlier (if you're following up with an email, send it as a reply to the initial one).

Keep it brief, and quickly make it clear why you're contacting them again. Most potential mentors are super busy, so don't waste their time by hiding the punch line three paragraphs into your email.

Initially, don't ask for anything (other than perhaps a meeting, if you haven't already met)—it's too early for that. Instead, look for a way to add value. If you can't find a way, don't contact them. Bide your time. For example, if the person is an investor, see if you can send them differentiated, insightful information about a stock they own (either your own analysis or an article/report they may not have seen). Or, in one page or less, outline a great new stock idea that's likely in their sweet spot. Or, you could simply send an article or analyst report that they're likely to find interesting.

It is always better to give than receive—but of course, the whole point of a mentor is that they can help you! That said, be very careful in asking for anything—even asking a question they'll feel obligated to reply to.

Nearly all of the emails I've sent to Buffett over two decades (roughly one per month) have been articles for which I don't expect a reply—rather, I'm just a clipping service, trying to be his eyes and ears, and only emailing him when I'm confident that I've found something that: a) is interesting and/or valuable; and b) he likely hasn't already seen.

If you ask for something, make sure you think they're very likely to say yes. People love to say yes to small asks and hate to say no.

Finally, you must always project the confidence that years from now, they are going to be delighted that they met you.

EXAMPLE OF A COMPELLING FOLLOW-UP

Here's a great example of a great follow-up email a young guy sent me:

> Whitney,
>
> Congratulations on the Value Investing Congress! It was a great learning experience, and I enjoyed it all around.
>
> All the invited speakers gave great presentations, and the opportunity to meet colleagues and make new friends with whom I share common interests is priceless.
>
> I just wanted to send you a quick thank you note since I can only imagine the time and effort that you must have placed in organizing the event.
>
> I look forward to seeing you at the next VIC in New York!
>
> Best,
>
> Francisco
>
> PS—My investment focus is mainly Mexico and Brazil; I will

email you whenever I find interesting investment opportunities in these countries.

You won't be surprised to hear that Francisco is now a close friend as well.

LONG-TERM RELATIONSHIP BUILDING

This final step, long-term relationship building, is the most important—not only for cultivating a mentor but deepening *all* relationships. Here's what has worked well for me:

- Be open, honest, and personal. Don't just talk about your achievements and what's going great in your life; also share setbacks and things that are causing you stress and keeping you up at night.
- When you open up to someone, it creates a level of intimacy that deepens the relationship and creates reciprocity, meaning they're likely to share personal stuff as well. You need to be careful, however—sharing too much too quickly can be perceived as inappropriate or even creepy. Seek balance in your relationships: you share something that's a little personal/intimate, then (hopefully) they reciprocate, and so forth until, over time, you can talk about anything. That's the hallmark of the kind of deep relationship you should strive for.
- Find common ground (again: college, kids, pets, sports,

travel, language, culture, etc.). If you run into a mutual friend, take a picture and send it with a nice note.

- Become their eyes and ears and send them articles and other materials of interest. But have a high bar—don't send too much!
- Congratulate them for something they did or that happened to them (you can set up Google alerts on anyone).
- Remember their birthdays, ideally with something special like an email with some photos of good times you've spent together.
- Invite them to a concert, game, or major life event like your birthday, wedding, bar mitzvah, etc. And, of course, if they invite you to anything, show up!
- If they hit you up for a charity, give (no matter how small)!
- Look for opportunities to do things with them—poker, golf, tennis, a trip, etc.
- Always pick up the tab when you're together. It shows generosity and creates reciprocity.
- Send an unexpected gift like a book or a bottle of wine.
- Surprise them with special, personal things like photos/photo albums, baby gifts (always a big hit!), and home-baked cookies. For example, every December, I bake chocolate chip cookies, put them in nice holiday tins, and send them to Buffett and Munger (they both have a sweet tooth), including our holiday card with a personal note thanking them for all they've taught me.
- Introduce them to someone. This only works, however,

if you're certain that it will be perceived as a valuable connection.

In two decades, I've only introduced Buffett to one person: tennis legend Billie Jean King. I met her at a private event at the US Open, and we had a nice conversation. I'm a lifelong tennis player and fan, so my knowledge of and interest in her was genuine.

Then, she asked me what I do. I said, "I'm a value investor, like Warren Buffett."

She exclaimed, "Oh, I love Warren Buffett!"

"Have you ever met him?" I inquired.

She said, "No, but I'd love to!"

"Well," I said, "I'm sure he'd love to meet you as well."

Buffett is a big sports fan—he loves rubbing elbows with stars like Alex Rodriguez, Tiger Woods, and LeBron James—so I immediately emailed his secretary and told her what was going on. Within minutes, she emailed me back and asked for King's mailing address.

Having made the connection, I didn't think of it again until, a decade later, I was having lunch with a friend who's close to Buffett and is a big tennis fan as well. I happened to tell him this story, and he laughed and said that not only did Buffett and King meet, but she now attends most Berkshire Hathaway annual meetings!

A NOTE ON PROFESSIONAL BUSINESS CORRESPONDENCE

If you're writing to a current or potential mentor, whether via letter, email, or text, don't be sloppy. It needs to be clear, concise, and well-written. If the person is older (like Buffett), you need to be at least somewhat formal. The salutation should be "Dear..." not "Hi..." and "Mr. Buffett," not "Warren." The first line might be something like, "It was a genuine pleasure speaking with you," not "It was great talking to you." And at the end, write "Sincerely yours," not "Best."

And beware of typos. The one that really drives me crazy is when someone tells me what a big fan they are of "Buffet" (it's Buffett!).

CONCLUSION

The quantity, quality, and depth of your relationships with others are likely to be the biggest drivers of your lifetime happiness. And, conversely, there are few things worse than a life of loneliness and ruptured relationships. So think hard about and invest in this area.

My goal is live my life in such a way that: a) I'm beloved while I'm alive; and b) When I die, they have to hold *two* services in the 1,200-seat sanctuary at Central Synagogue (to which my family and I belong) because there are so many mentors, friends, and people I've touched who want to mourn me and give eulogies!

A BAD MARRIAGE, OFTEN ENDING IN DIVORCE

Buffett once said that the two most important decisions you make in your life are who you marry and what career you choose.

I agree.

Regarding marriage, based on my own 27 years of experience, a lifetime of observation, and quite a bit of research (which, for example, reveals that one-third of marriages are severely strained), I can't think of anything more important to long-term happiness than a strong marriage. It's the most important relationship in your life.

Until about 10 years ago, this wasn't something I thought

much about because divorces among my friends and family were extremely rare. But since then, it's been an epidemic. More than a dozen people I'm close to have gone through a divorce, and in every case, it's been a nightmare.

So initially, the title of this chapter was going to be: "Calamity #3: Divorce." But then Susan pointed out that the real calamity isn't the divorce—in fact, that's often the relief valve. It's the many years of misery *prior* to the divorce that's the real calamity.

You can see this in these charts based on a global survey showing life satisfaction, for both men and women, in the five years before and after divorce:[1]

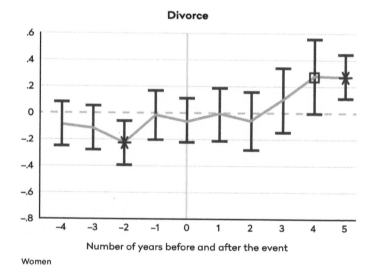

Divorce

Number of years before and after the event

Women

1   Ortiz-Ospina, Esteban, and Max Roser. "Happiness and Life Satisfaction." *Our World in Data*, May 2017, https://ourworldindata.org/happiness-and-life-satisfaction.

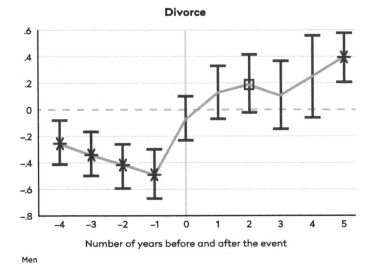

Divorce

Number of years before and after the event

Men

For both men and women, life satisfaction is negative in the years leading up to a divorce but then turns positive afterward (with men experiencing much stronger and more rapid effects, both negative and then positive).

Having a good marriage is a function of two things: marrying the right person and maintaining a healthy relationship with them.

MARRYING THE RIGHT PERSON

I love the advice Charlie Munger gave when asked for the key to marrying a great person: look in a mirror and try to improve yourself because great people only marry other great people.

Once you establish criteria to evaluate a potential spouse, ask yourself how you stack up on those same criteria. There are always things to work on, and constantly improving is a great way to attract a wonderful spouse (and be successful in life!).

You never know where you might meet that perfect person, but there are certainly some places where you're more—or less—likely to do so.

I met Susan in September 1990 when a friend and I crashed the Harvard Law School orientation boat cruise on Boston Harbor. That was a good place to look.

One of my friends met his wife when he volunteered to guide blind runners in the New York City marathon. What a great place to meet people, as everyone there was highly likely to be both athletic and good-hearted.

In contrast, a Navy SEAL told me he met his wife at a strip club where she was performing. Later, as he was thinking of marrying her, he said his friends told him that as soon as he was deployed overseas, she'd cheat on him and empty his bank account. He ruefully admitted that that's exactly what happened.

Once you're actively improving yourself and looking in the right places, you need to have good evaluation criteria. I've been thinking about this for years and have come up with numerous questions that I think anyone should ask when considering whether to marry someone. I've boiled them down to a dozen, listed in rough order of importance.

THE 12 QUESTIONS TO ASK BEFORE YOU MARRY SOMEONE

1) Are they a warm, kind, and good-hearted person, both toward you and others? Do they have a mean bone in their body? How do they treat people like employees, waiters, and taxi drivers? Do children and dogs like them?

This is so important—and it's so easy to be fooled because, of course, the person you're dating is going to be on their best behavior around you. That's why it's critical to watch how they treat others, especially those they don't perceive to be peers. Children and dogs are often much better judges of character than you are!

2) If you weren't romantically interested in each other, would you be close friends? Do you make each other better?

Over time, when the passion and romance aren't so intense, there had better be a solid foundation of friendship, or you're in trouble. You want to be with someone who gives you frank feedback and smooths your rough edges—as Susan regularly does with me!

3) Do they have high integrity? Are they a stable, solid, predictable person who you can count on 100%? Do you trust them completely? Are there any issues with anger management, violence, narcissism, alcohol, or drugs?

There can be no compromise in this area. If you don't trust someone with your life—if you're not 100,000% certain that they would never cheat on you or knowingly hurt you, directly or indirectly, in any way—then RUN! If you find yourself rationalizing, "Well, he's great most of the time, but sometimes when he's had too much to drink..." RUN!

One of my friends who's dated a lot of people told me that many of them can't "relax and be themselves" until they've had many drinks. If you observe this, RUN!

4) Do you share core values, e.g., self-improvement, giving back/philanthropy, meritocracy, humility, life balance, spirituality, thinking before acting, looking for win-win solutions?

Every person's list here will be different. I thought about adding "political views," but you'll have to decide that for yourself.

5) Are they intelligent and intellectually curious? Do you find them interesting?

This isn't code for "did they attend an elite college?" My dad is from a prominent family in Connecticut and went to a private high school before attending Yale, while my mom is the daughter of a Seattle fireman and went to public schools all the way through the University of Washington. So what? They're both smart, intellectually curious, and interesting—and have been happily married for more than 58 years!

6) Do they like to do fun things and have a zest for life? Are they a happy and optimistic person? Do they have a good sense of humor and make you laugh?

There are so many people who look great on paper—they're nice, went to a good school, have a solid job, etc.—but are just, well...boring. You don't want to be married to someone like that unless that's what you're looking for, of course!

7) Do they have a strong work ethic and a purpose?

Initially, this question was "Do they have a good job or career," but I changed it because some people choose to do things like write books, raise kids, or do volunteer work—and they're very happy and are wonderful spouses. The point of this question is that if you're a driven person and your spouse is a lump, your marriage isn't likely to last.

8) Do they come from a stable family? Do you want to spend time with them (because you will!)?

The first part of the question here is tricky because it seems unfair to hold it against someone if they happen to come from a messed up family. But I'll be honest: I'd rather see my daughters marry guys whose families are similar to ours—filled with deep, long-term, loving relationships.

9) Do your friends and family like them?

Similar to the dogs and children question, someone may be able to fool you...but they're unlikely to be able to fool all of your friends and family. Ask people close to you what they think—and listen carefully!

10) Do they have similar views on big issues such as where to live, children (how many, what religion, how will child-rearing duties be split), whether one of you will stop or cut back on working to raise the kids, and finances (spending habits, lifestyle, debt, the importance of having a lot of money)? Will they be a good parent?

As your relationship deepens, you'll want to think about these things—and have some conversations about them, however difficult that might be.

Regarding religion, I remember on my first date with my

wife, I told her we could raise our kids Jewish. It was certainly premature—I said it with a smile—but it's a critical conversation to have if you and your potential spouse are from different religions. (I wasn't raised religious, so it wasn't a sacrifice for me—and I'm delighted that my daughters are Jewish, as I fully embrace the values of the religion.)

Another huge issue is balancing both of your careers with the demands of raising a family. A lot of guys have the sexist assumption that their wives will sacrifice their careers once kids come along, which can lead to anger, resentment, and eventually, divorce.

11) Have they had long-term relationships in the past? How have they ended? What would previous boyfriends or girlfriends say about them?

When deciding whether to raise children and spend the rest of your life with someone, you should be less concerned with how someone is 99% of the time than with how their worst 1% looks like. Observing or talking to ex-partners is a good place to start.

12) Do you think they're attractive, and do you have a wild, passionate sex life?

A good sex life is an important element of a healthy marriage, but I have deliberately listed this as the last and least important question in part because so many young people seem to put it first. I know a number of guys who are trapped in miserable marriages with women who are mean, shallow, or otherwise unpleasant—but, boy, were they hot and sexy when they were younger! To quote the old adage, these guys let their little heads think for their big ones...and have been paying a big price ever since.

I am not saying that you need a perfect answer to every one of these questions. Every person might have a slightly different set of questions, prioritize them differently, and think differently about what flaws can be overlooked. For example, can you live with someone who occasionally smokes marijuana? Or has very different political beliefs? Or spends money more freely than you? What if you want to raise the kids in your faith, but your potential spouse wants to let them decide for themselves? There are no easy answers to questions like this.

A guy I met recently asked me an interesting question:

> "Once you've gone on a few dates with someone you like, is there a way to accelerate finding the answers to the 12 questions? The cost of waiting when the answer ends up being "no" is that you've lost time you could have spent looking for the right partner.
>
> One strategy I've heard of is going on camping trips together

early in a relationship, where something inevitably goes wrong, and you can see how the other person reacts."

Here was my reply: I would worry less about how much time it takes to really get to know someone, and more about staying with someone you know isn't right, out of inertia or "he/she is really nice" or "wow, the sex is great." Worse yet, if you let it drag on long enough, you might just marry this wrong person—I've seen it happen. So keep in mind what Bill Gates once said of employees: "Hire slowly; fire quickly."

Another friend asked if I thought the decision to marry someone should be based on some variation of my 12 questions or on gut instinct?

I think both. Any relationship has to start with genuine, emotional attraction. Don't even think about these questions until it becomes more serious, and you're asking yourself, "Is this the person I want to spend the rest of my life with?"

But then, be sure to ask these questions because it might help you avoid a terrible mistake. Someone close to me is twice divorced—and both times, I'm convinced that, had she had this list, she wouldn't have married either dud. Sometimes the smartest people make the dumbest decisions when it comes to matters of the heart.

That said, once you've asked—and, more importantly—honestly answered the questions, then what do you do? Let's say you assign each question a score of one, a half, or zero. If you give the person you're dating a score of eight, that's clearly not good enough—keep looking. On the other hand, you're likely to never get married if you hold out for a perfect 12. But what if your score is 10—is that good enough? I can't answer that for you. Ultimately, the final decision is yours—and one of the heart, not the head.

But don't make a quick decision or rush into anything. This is a decision you must get right, so be careful, take your time, and don't compromise.

Nobody is perfect, but if you're not 99% certain that you want to spend the rest of your life with this person, then wait, collect more information, and do more thinking.

BE WILLING TO WALK

During the romantic whirlwind of dating, you might get fooled, so be on the lookout for warning flags, and if you're having serious second thoughts, don't hesitate to call things off, even if it's the day before the wedding. In fact, it's between the engagement and the wedding that your soon-to-be-spouse, thinking the deal is sealed, might let down their guard and show their true colors.

This is exactly what happened to one of my friends. I met his girlfriend and then a few months later heard the wonderful news that they'd gotten engaged and set a wedding date. As the big day approached, I called him to ask about the schedule for the weekend so I could plan my flights so as not to miss any pre- or post-wedding activities.

But I was surprised when he instead said, "Whitney, I'm having second thoughts..."

"Why?" I asked.

"Two things. First, a few weeks after we got engaged, she told me the diamond in the engagement ring I'd bought her wasn't big enough."

"Uh, oh," I said. "What else?"

"When I told her that I'm providing financial support to my parents, who aren't doing so well, she made it clear that she didn't want me to continue doing so after we were married."

"Wow," I said. "I hate to be judgmental, but either one of those two things would be instant deal-breakers for me. She's done you a huge favor by showing you this side of herself before you're married and before you have kids..."

Sure enough, a week later, he told me he called off the marriage. It was the right call. Now, a few years later, he just got married—and couldn't be happier.

As Maya Angelou once said, "When someone shows you who they are, believe them the first time."

In investing, there's a trap called commitment bias, meaning that, once you own a stock, especially if you've written or talked about it publicly, your natural inclination is to become committed to it, such that your mind blocks out new, disconfirming information. This can lead to disastrous results. To offset this, you must make a conscious effort to not only be open to but actively seek out information that would cause you to change your mind.

Ditto for a romantic relationship—up to the point of marriage, at least. It's wonderful to fall in love, but the swirl of passion, romance, and emotions can lead to a terrible, life-altering decision to marry the wrong person. So try to retain a bit of rationality, honestly ask and answer the questions above and, even if you're engaged, have booked the venue, ordered the food and flowers, etc., call off (or at least delay) the wedding if you realize you might be making a mistake. It's hard to break off an engagement, but being in a bad marriage (usually followed by divorce) is light-years worse!

MAINTAINING A HEALTHY MARRIAGE

When a marriage fails, it's easy to assume that it was doomed from the beginning. But my observation is that in more than half of the divorces I've seen, the couple was compatible, and their marriage started off well—let's call it an eight or more on a scale of one to ten. But then, often over a decade or more, it slowly declined to a six, then a four, then a two, then BOOM!

How did these once-happy marriages fall apart? I've studied this question carefully for many years because I really, really, really don't want it to happen to me!

I'm pleased to say that, after being together for 30 years and married more than twenty-seven, Susan's and my marriage has gotten better with age, which is remarkable and wonderful. It's due, to some extent, to writing a slide presentation and, now, this book on the subject of maintaining a healthy marriage. It's made me more aware of my behavior toward Susan—there was, and still is, lots of room for improvement—and triggered many good conversations that otherwise might not have occurred.

Usually, when people think about a marriage falling apart, they think about something dramatic—infidelity, violence, criminal behavior, alcoholism—that suddenly ruptures the relationship.

Among the marriages I've observed that have gone bad, however, not a single one ended suddenly. Rather, they disintegrated slowly and painfully over many years.

In most cases, I don't think it was irreversible. Instead, a number of things happened that put pressure on the marriage, causing what was once an eight to slip to a six. Maybe having children or dealing with an aging parent led to stress. Or one spouse began to travel a lot for work, while the other stopped working to care for the kids, so they started living increasingly separate lives. Or they just started getting sloppy in their behavior toward each other—being short-tempered, leaving dirty laundry or dishes around, not helping out with routine childcare and chores—which let anger and resentment start to build.

This is a critical time because, while a six isn't a healthy, happy marriage, it's not a miserable, irrecoverable one either. Susan and I have fallen to this level a few times.

The key here is whether the couple a) recognizes that their marriage has fallen into the danger zone; b) communicates openly and honestly about it; and c) takes steps to address the problem(s) and get their marriage back into the healthy eight-plus range. Thankfully, we were able to do these things.

You might think that the first step—awareness—is easy, but

it's not. Friends of mine have been completely blindsided when their wife came home and said she wanted a divorce. It's important not only to regularly ask yourself how healthy *you* think your marriage is but also to ask your spouse!

This doesn't come naturally to many folks, so when I'm presenting this to a live audience, I ask the following:

- Raise your hand if you're married
- Keep your hand up if having a healthy, happy, long-lasting marriage is really important to you (nobody ever lowers a hand)
- Keep your hand up if you would rate your marriage, on a scale of one to ten an eight or better—and you're confident that your spouse would as well (many hands go down)
- For those of you who lowered your hand, put it back up if you're confident that you and your spouse are communicating well and are working effectively together to get your marriage up to at least an eight (few go back up)
- If you didn't just raise your hand, what is stopping you from having a conversation soon about how to improve your marriage? (The answer, of course, is nothing.)

So let's talk about the things that can place stress on a marriage.

DAY-TO-DAY BEHAVIOR TOWARD EACH OTHER

It's sad that we often treat our spouses in ways we would never dream of treating our friends. Why? Because, consciously or subconsciously, we know that if we treat friends badly, we'll lose them. But spouses—at least in the short run—aren't likely to walk away.

So it's easy to get sloppy and lazy and forget to treat our spouses with patience, forgiveness, kindness, love, and fairness.

In a *New York Times* article, one couple described what happened to them:

> "With all my energy going into the kids, I didn't have much leftover for Frank," she said.

> What pushed them apart?

> For six years, they drifted. Her drive for intimacy was gone. They had spells where they connected, but they were inconsistent about making time for each other. "We fell out of love with each other, and I think we were both sad about it," she said. More than once, he said to her, "You always think the worst of me."

> She agreed. "I took him for granted; I was harsh and said things that were critical," she said. "My patience was worn thin, and I was snappy and wasn't very forgiving."

"I thought someday sex would come back; I was in denial that we were running on fumes, but it was hard to feel sexual after taking care of the kids all day and I didn't know what to do or how to fix it," she said.

Above all, beware of what renowned marriage researcher John Gottman calls the Four Horsemen of the Apocalypse: criticism, contempt, defensiveness, and stonewalling. I've seen all of these—though fortunately not often between Susan and me—and they're deadly! Left unchecked, they will undo even good marriages.

Instead, as the old saying goes, "If you want to be loved, be lovable." I remember at the funeral of one of my investors, his wife said something so beautiful, simple, and powerful that I've never forgotten it: "Every day, he made me feel loved." So hold hands, hug and kiss a lot, and try to regularly earn goodwill so that when you screw up (you will!), your spouse forgives you. It's not only a good way to maintain a healthy marriage, but a smart way to live your life in general!

KIDS

There are many potential areas of friction when it comes to raising kids because it requires countless difficult and emotional decisions: who feeds and takes care of the young ones, who sets behavior boundaries, how to discipline them, when they get a smartphone, how much TV/screen time is allowed, etc.

Having kids strengthened Susan's and my marriage. It was a shared activity that brought us together—plus, I usually deferred to her in this area because I recognized that she's a lot better at parenting than I am!

But studies show that we're the exception, as children tend to put a strain on marriages. Here are the relevant charts for both women and men, which show that life satisfaction declines after the birth of a child—and never fully recovers[2]:

Birth of Child

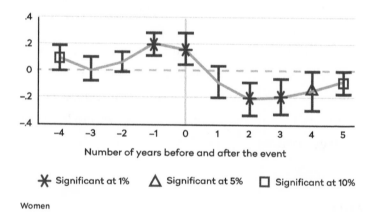

Women

<hr />

2   Ortiz-Ospina, Esteban, and Max Roser. "Happiness and Life Satisfaction." *Our World in Data*, May 2017, https://ourworldindata.org/happiness-and-life-satisfaction.

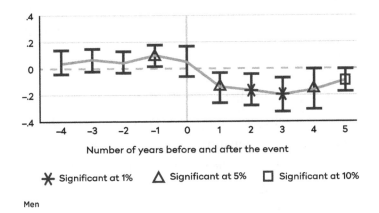

Men

I think a major reason women's life satisfaction dips is that they end up assuming most of the childcare duties, which often leads to anger and resentment. According to one study, in the 1960s, women spent 3.4 times more time every day doing child or adult (elderly) care than their husbands. While it had declined to 1.9 times in the period of 2010-15, that's still a grossly unfair ratio, so, to the fathers reading this, get off your butts and start pitching in more! (And to the mothers, help us out by being very clear about how we can be helpful—a lot of this stuff doesn't come naturally to us!)

Couples married before 1992 seemed satisfied to have the wife do most of the housework and childcare. But that has changed. Studies in 2006 found that the happiest and most sexually satisfied couples are now those who divide housework and childcare the most equally.

I'll admit that I didn't come within a country mile of doing my fair share of raising our daughters. Susan really knew and connected with them on a deep level, knew their friends and teachers, etc.

But I did one thing that was helpful. Every Saturday and Sunday, I took the girls into Central Park for all-day "Daddy Olympics." I'd be pushing the double jogger, wearing my rollerblades, and, depending on their age, the girls were sitting in the stroller, on scooters (starting at age 18 months), or riding bikes (I removed the training wheels at age three). The stroller was filled with soccer balls, frisbees, bats, and balls, and we'd go around the park, stopping at our favorite fields, playgrounds, the merry-go-round, rock-climbing area, and zoo. Here's a picture of us (along with Susan, Dana, and my parents) about to go out on one of our expeditions:

And here's one a few years later:

It was a win-win-win-win: it was fun; it helped me build strong relationships with my daughters; Susan got a much-needed break, and it helped turn my girls into super-confident athletes.

The latter was really important to me because of two surveys I'd read. The first asked young girls a simple yet fundamental question: "Do you like yourself?" 80% of 12-year-olds said yes. But only two years later, this number crashed to 30% due, I suspect, to advertising, social pressure to be super skinny, and an idealized version of beauty.

To combat this, I wanted my girls to have enormous egos going into their teenage years, and I figured one way to do this would be to have them be adventurous, outdoorsy, and athletic (in contrast to the many "indoor kids" so common in New York City). So during our Central Park adventures, I pushed them outside of their comfort zones.

When they were only a few months old, I strapped them into the jogging stroller (with helmets!), put on my roller-blades, and we went whizzing around the park at high speed. At every playground, I put them in my lap, and we went down the tallest slides, swung on the highest swings, and rode the biggest horses on the merry-go-round. Then, at a ridiculously young age, I made them do it by themselves.

I remember one time when Emily was maybe 18 months

old. We went to the merry-go-round, but rather than sitting on the big horse with her, I plunked her on, wrapped the big leather belt twice around her tiny waist, and stood next to her. As the ride started to move and the horse began to go up and down, maybe three feet at a time, she was scared and started crying and clutching for me. But I put her hands back on the pole and told her to hang on. She howled—but soon saw she could do it by herself. The next time, she was happy to ride alone while I rode the horse next to her.

Another of my favorite games was climbing with my little girls to the top of the slide, but then putting them on it by themselves, with me standing on the ladder behind. The first time, they were super scared and wanted to climb back down, but I wouldn't let them and told them that if they didn't go on their own, I was going to push them. They knew I wasn't kidding, so down they went.

They quickly realized that they could do all of these things by themselves—and it was fun!

Of course, there were plenty of falls and scraped knees, but when they came crying to me, I woudn't coddle them. One time Emily came crying to me with a boo-boo on her finger. I examined it and, seeing that it wasn't serious, announced in a loud voice, "Alison, get a knife!" All of the other parents gasped as I continued, "We're going to amputate!" I started sawing at Emily's finger with my hand. She started giggling and was soon back to playing.

There was an added benefit to all of this: I'd read a study that revealed that girls who played varsity sports in high school got better grades and were far less likely to get into various types of trouble like eating disorders, drug use, and promiscuity.

Needless to say, my girls all played multiple varsity sports, navigated their teenage years well (Katharine still has a couple of years to go), and are thriving.

RISK OF DIVORCE RISES WHEN YOUR YOUNGEST CHILD REACHES ADOLESCENCE

This is purely anecdotal, but my observation is that the risk of divorce rises when the youngest child reaches adolescence. I think this is due to two primary factors: one causation and the other correlation.

First, raising young children is often very fulfilling for parents—it's something they can do together. But by adolescence, children are more independent—so raising them may become less of a team effort—and more difficult to manage, which can lead to conflict between the parents.

Second, parents who are unhappy with their marriage often

stay together for the sake of young children. But by adolescence, one or both parents may feel that the children can handle their parents' divorce, so they finally initiate what had perhaps become inevitable years earlier.

FIDELITY/INFIDELITY

Fidelity is like virginity: it's relatively easy to maintain, but once lost, it's impossible to restore.

The surest way to end your marriage is to cheat on your spouse. Even if you don't get caught, it'll mess with your head and make divorce far more likely.

Sometimes, infidelity occurs in an unplanned way: you get drunk in the wrong place at the wrong time, like a bachelor party in Las Vegas. (Note: what happens in Vegas does not usually stay in Vegas!)

More often, it's not a momentary lapse of judgment but a consensual affair. It usually begins with flirting that appears harmless but then gradually escalates.

There's a simple way to avoid this: don't flirt, ever!

Absolutely no good can come of it. Think about it: either the person you're flirting with welcomes it, in which case you're on the slippery slope to an affair, a ruined marriage, and divorce, or the person doesn't welcome it and thinks you're creepy and gross. Why would you engage in this lose-lose proposition?

The answer, of course, is that it can be fun to flirt, and it's flattering when someone shows a romantic interest in you. It never ceases to amaze me how many married people flirt. They're like horny teenagers who can't control themselves. Maybe they tell themselves it's harmless and rationalize, "All I did was tell her she looks hot in that dress. I'm not planning on sleeping with her!" Most of the time, they're right—it probably is harmless. But it's still dumb, so don't do it!

My mom often says, "If you never go to first base with flirting, there's no chance that you'll arrive at the home plate of infidelity."

SEX

There's an old joke about the guy who goes into the drug store and asks the pharmacist why condoms come in three-packs, six-packs, and 12-packs. He replies, "The three-packs are for teenagers: Thursday, Friday, and Saturday. The six-packs are for young adults: Monday, Tuesday, Wednesday, Thursday, Friday, and Saturday. The 12-packs are for married couples: January, February, March..."

It's hard to tell whether a declining sex life is a symptom

or a cause of a bad marriage, but I can't think of a single instance of someone saying: "My marriage went bad, but our sex life remained great until the end."

Instead, what usually happens is that the sex life (both frequency and satisfaction) mirrors the health of the marriage overall.

Studies show that in the early days of wooing, engagement, and marriage, couples are having sex a few times a week, but then this drops to about once a week for the average American couple.

There's no "right" frequency, and every couple is different, but here are two thoughts: first, if you're dissatisfied with your sex life for whatever reason, you must figure out a way to have a conversation with your spouse about it, however difficult this might be. If left unaddressed, it can undermine an otherwise healthy marriage.

Second, if your sex life has dried up—if, say, it was once a week for many years, but over the past year or two has dwindled to only twice or even once a month—worry! It doesn't mean for sure that your marriage is on the rocks, but there's a good chance that it's indicative of a weakening marriage. Think about it: sex is wildly fun and pleasurable, so why would your spouse want to have less of it with you? The possible answers are mostly bad news, so do not ignore this warning flag! Again, the key is communication, however uncomfortable.

(Phew! Got through that part while adhering to Susan's admonition: "Do not use personal anecdotes!" LOL!)

COMMON ACTIVITIES

One of my friends told me that his marriage ended soon after his career took off, which led him to travel frequently while his wife stopped working to stay home and raise their kids. They began leading such different lives that they eventually became, he said, "like two ships passing in the night."

To ensure that this doesn't happen to you, look for things that you and your spouse can enjoy together. Here are some things Susan and I do:

- We do things with our daughters, both little (family dinner most nights) and big (vacationing together as often as we can)
- We have some favorite TV shows we always watch together, such as the late-night comedy shows (Trevor Noah, Seth Meyers, etc.) and—confession time!—*Survivor* and *The Amazing Race* (we've never missed an episode of either in nearly two decades)
- Every week or two, we go to a movie or show together (at least we used to before the pandemic!)

- We walk our beloved Rosie (the Wonder Dog) most
  mornings

I'm totally serious when I say that Rosie has been good for
our marriage! Here's a picture of us:

Other couples have a designated "date night" every week
(you can do it at home, just make it special and intentional),
or exercise or play a sport like golf together.

THE LITTLE THINGS

Lastly, don't forget the little things. It's so easy to stop paying attention and get sloppy with things like leaving the toilet seat up, being smelly, waking up your spouse when going to bed or getting up, hogging the blanket, leaving dirty clothes or dishes lying around, etc.

Each one, by itself, is insignificant. But anyone who knows horses will tell you that even one burr under the saddle, left unattended, can chafe, turn into a sore, and eventually kill a horse. Ditto for a marriage.

WRITING THIS BOOK

Writing this chapter was good for my marriage because, as I was writing it, I'd read parts of it to Susan—and sometimes get an earful in return! For example, when I wrote about the importance of paying attention to the little things, I recall her exploding, saying, "You $#@&*%$ hypocrite—you're out there telling other people to listen to their spouses and pick up after themselves, but you're not doing it yourself!"

She was right, of course. By getting all of the issues raised in this chapter out on the table, we had some frank—and, yes, sometimes uncomfortable—discussions that we otherwise might not have had, and our marriage is the better for it.

HOW MAKING A LOT OF MONEY INCREASES THE ODDS OF DIVORCE

Most people think that making a lot of money strengthens a marriage. Up to a certain point, that's true, as financial pressures can strain a marriage.

But, counterintuitively, I've seen seven ways of how making a significant amount of money can actually *increase* the odds of divorce:

1) Divorce is crazy expensive, so having a lot of money removes this barrier.

There is both the short-term cost of lawyers and the long-term higher expenses due to two homes, less favorable tax treatment, etc. I know one guy whose wife suddenly inherited a huge amount of money—and told him that very night that she wanted a divorce. My wife and I joke (at least I hope she's joking!) that, even if we wanted to, we couldn't afford to get divorced. Even though it's not technically true, I'm glad she thinks it is!

2) Odds of infidelity go up.

Making a lot of money generally requires working long hours and, often, a lot of travel, which can put a huge strain on a marriage and increase opportunities for infidelity (both for the person traveling and for the one at home). Also, rich people are more likely to attract those interested in having an affair. Lastly, wealth equals power, which some people exploit for sexual advantage.

3) When a couple is scraping and hustling to make ends meet, it's a bonding experience.

When you're both young and working to support yourselves (and, eventually, a family), it can be stressful but also joyful and unifying. You're both in the same boat, leading similar, parallel lives.

4) It can change the power dynamic in the marriage.

When both of you are earning roughly the same amount, there's symmetry and equality. If that shifts, it can lead the high-earner—even if subconsciously—to feel a sense of superiority, lose respect for the spouse, and/or expect him or her to do more of the housework/childcare—in short, a recipe for marital strife.

5) If one person makes enough money that their spouse can stop working, it can eventually lead to deep unhappiness for the nonworking spouse.

I'll acknowledge up front that this is a high-class problem that pretty much only affects one-percenters—but that's my world. See my friends' comments on this below.

6) Deciding how to spend (or not spend) the newfound wealth can lead to conflict.

One friend told me that when he hit it big, he couldn't wait to spend his fortune and enjoy the luxuries of life. For example, he wanted to live in a big brownstone in New York City and have a mansion in the Hamptons.

But his wife was super frugal, uncomfortable with their new wealth, and even more uncomfortable displaying it. He ignored her wishes and went ahead with his purchases, which he believes was a major contributor to their divorce a few years later.

7) Becoming very rich can change people for the worse: they can become arrogant and self-absorbed and look down on others.

Just open the newspaper to see examples of rich, narcissistic jerks everywhere, like Tesla CEO Elon Musk or Uber co-founder Travis Kalanick. But were they always this way, or did making a ton of money cause them to become so? My observation of dozens of extremely wealthy people is that it's 25% causation and 75% inflammation.

Regarding the former, if you make a lot of money, people start to suck up to you...and it's easy to come to believe that you're smarter, taller, funnier, better-looking, and more charming than you really are, which can lead to all sorts of bad behavior.

Regarding the latter, making a lot of money doesn't so much change people as inflame their preexisting tendencies. If they were a jerk when they had no money, they're likely to be an even bigger jerk after they make a lot of money.

But, conversely, some people improve. Becoming financially secure reduces their stress level, and they have the ability to help others, which can bring them joy.

I'm quite certain that I'm a much better human being now than I was 30 years ago in my twenties when I had almost no savings and plenty of student loans. I'm biased, of course, but I think I'm wiser, more self-aware, kinder, more philanthropic, a better listener, and more humble (though there's still a lot of room for improvement in every one of these areas!).

How much of this is due to becoming financially secure? Maybe a little, though I think most of it is having a learning curve that slopes upward (however slightly), the positive effect Susan has had on me, and the knowledge I've absorbed from Buffett and Munger.

"A TOTAL EPIDEMIC OF LOST WOMEN"

I want to share some thoughts about a crisis I've observed among many wealthy, well-educated women. (I have never shared these thoughts publicly because some people will no doubt view them as sexist, and I have no data to back this up—they're just my anecdotal observations.)

Let me start by making the politically incorrect statement that, in most cases I've seen, it's the husband who starts making big money and the wife who stops working, usually when kids arrive.

She becomes a stay-at-home mom, and, initially, everything is wonderful. She throws herself into motherhood, which is a full-time job when one or more little children need constant attention.

But then the kids start school, which results in large blocks of free time during the day. How to occupy this time? Keep in mind that these are highly educated, capable women who, five to 15 years earlier, had demanding, high-paying jobs. But good luck finding anything similar to that, given the long absence from the workforce and the inability/unwillingness to work long hours or travel.

Another factor here is that the husband may not be supportive. One divorced female friend told me:

"When we got married, I had a high-powered job and he was still in graduate school. But then he started working and his career took off, which became his primary focus.

By the time we had our first child, he was earning quite a bit more than I was, so I decided to stop working temporarily. Our roles had reversed, and it really changed the power dynamic between us—a concept I had never even contemplated.

Two years (and one more child) later, when I wanted to go back to work full time, he made it clear to me that he wasn't willing to make any adjustments to his career to help with the kids, so it was up to me to figure out how to balance any job I took with properly caring for and raising our two young children. There are only 24 hours in a day, so I ended up only being able to take a part-time job, which has really affected my career.

Did I resent him for this? You bet! It was certainly a major factor in the end of our marriage years later.

In retrospect, I really regret not standing up for myself more. I tell the many young women I supervise and mentor not to give up their power and their dreams/aspirations.

They need to have a conversation with their partner *before* they get married about what their expectations, needs, and demands are regarding balancing their careers and future families. If they want to have both children and demanding careers, then they need to make sure to marry someone who will be supportive of that, even if it requires them to make personal and career sacrifices."

Some mothers don't go back to work full time because their husbands aren't supportive, but others choose not to. They may be delighted to get out of the corporate rat race, with its long hours, heavy travel, and, often, sexism.

Some—perhaps even most—find genuine happiness and fulfillment.

But not all...

And here's the problem: it can be hard to tell the difference— even, sometimes, to the women themselves.

From the outside, both the happy and unhappy stay-at-home moms may appear to have wonderful lives: perfect children, perfect homes, perfect fitness, perfect vacations, and perfect charitable endeavors.

But for some wives, boredom may creep in. Consciously or subconsciously, they may feel a lack of meaning in their lives. Over time, this can lead to deep unhappiness, even depression, and an acute midlife crisis that can blow up a marriage. One of my (female) friends called the situation "a total epidemic of lost women."

Another straight-shooting female friend wrote:

> "Most of my acquaintances married to uber-rich guys still work. I never understood why women would get multiple Ivy League degrees to retire at 33.
>
> The ones who don't are often CEOs of their house, compulsive shoppers, and causing misery—bossing people around—at the private schools their children attend or the charities they volunteer at.
>
> There are plenty of miserable "ladies who lunch" for sure. I usually see them at boutique fitness classes, yoga, etc. Most aren't divorced (yet), but a lot of sexless marriages for sure.
>
> Of those who have gotten divorced, their husbands often cheated on them.
>
> The wives are much happier now. They've had to go back to work, but typically not at their old law firm or Wall Street jobs—they're working at schools or other nonprofits, doing social work, therapy, interior design, etc.
>
> The periods when I have not worked in a fulfilling job have been the most challenging ones for my marriage. I am at my

best as a wife (and mom and person!) when I'm happy at work."

My observation is that the husband is often completely oblivious to what is happening. He has a fulfilling career in which he interacts with lots of interesting people, regularly travels to new places, and solves engaging challenges. And at home, things seem fine—the kids are thriving, and there are no big spousal conflicts. Maybe the spark is gone, and sex has dwindled, but hey, that's just what happens after you've been married for a while, right?

Maybe...but maybe not. In some cases, before they know it, tick...tick...BOOM! Welcome to divorce, which is always miserable, but is an especially awful nightmare when big money and kids are involved...

Another (happily married) female friend observed:

"I think it would be nice if there were a one-size-fits-all rule book for happy marriages, but I don't think that that is possible. What works for us does not work for our friends. And what works for us today would not have worked for us 10 years ago.

I don't think that a woman's employment status is generally at the heart of marital unhappiness among the very wealthy. Some of my friends are bored at home, some completely fulfilled. Some of my friends are overly stressed by work, others completely fulfilled.

Unlike your other 'straight-shooting' friend, I know tons of well-educated women who do not work and do not go around 'causing misery.' Simultaneously, I know women, and men, who have huge jobs and still manage to find the time to go around, causing misery.

Your friend's example of women who volunteer in their children's schools sounds nasty and does not ring true to me. My three friends who were super-volunteers at their children's private schools were capable lawyers and businesspeople who were so cherished that they were eventually hired by the schools (like Susan!). Also, my own children's school is full of women who started volunteering decades ago, and the school has never let go of them.

I, too, have seen many women who would rather 'do good' than 'do well' once they can afford to make that choice. I think this is a sign of self-awareness, which I don't often see in uber-rich/successful men.

Unlike you, I do not see my friends' ex-husbands (or soon-to-be ex-husbands) as fulfilled, happy-go-lucky men. Many of my friends report that their husbands were (for years, even decades) unhappy. They found it 'lonely at the top' and suffered from so much stress and anxiety that they could not sleep past 4 a.m. It is this (tired and grumpy) man who is less desirable as a sex partner...and life partner.

If I were to give your uber-rich friends advice on how to save their marriages, I would be more inclined to say that they need to work on figuring out what makes themselves happy first. Then, being nice to their wives, maybe even thoughtful, might be better advice than telling them to tell that bum-of-a-wife of theirs to 'Go get a job!' Maybe they should be thinking to themselves, 'Wow, if I stop being a dick to my wife and sleeping with other women, I might be able to have a happy marriage after all!'"

What wise friends I have!

In conclusion, forgive me if what I've written here offends you. But maybe it will help at least one of my readers, who says, "Boy, this hit awfully close to home. Maybe I should reflect on my behavior and have a conversation with my spouse..."

HOW DIVORCE CAN AFFECT YOUR WORK

Lastly, as if you need any additional reasons to avoid divorce, it can really affect your performance at work for four reasons:

1. It sucks up a huge amount of time;

2. It sucks up even more mental energy and creates stress;
3. It creates huge financial pressure, which can lead to reckless, swing-for-the-fences decisions; and
4. After separation, resuming a dating life occupies the mind, consumes huge amounts of time, and (let's be honest) often leads to extreme sleep deprivation.

SHOULD YOU GET DIVORCED?

This is one of the hardest questions anyone has to face, and you are well-advised to ask a professional therapist, not me. But I will share some of the many factors to consider:

- How miserable are you, really?
- How likely are you to be happier after you get divorced? (I've seen many people have a midlife crisis and initiate a divorce based on a delusion that it will lead to happiness, but instead, they make things much worse for themselves, their ex, and their children.)
- Is there any possibility that things will improve? Have you tried everything to address what's making you unhappy and give your spouse (and yourself!) every opportunity to change?
- Do you have kids? What will be the impact on them?
- What are the financial implications? If you've been out of the workforce for many years, finding a good job may be difficult.

Call me old-school, but I believe that people should do their absolute best to adhere to their marriage vows. Divorce should be an absolute last resort.

That said, if you're truly miserable and don't think things are likely to change, get out. Even at age 50, you still have nearly half of your life left—and I know many people who have found their soulmate and tremendous happiness in their second marriage.

CALAMITY #4

===

ADDICTION AND ABUSE

There are so many ways that addictive/abusive behaviors can get you into trouble, ruin your life, and even kill you. In this chapter, I cover some of the big ones.

ALCOHOL ABUSE

When I order a Diet Coke while others are drinking wine or having a beer, I'm sometimes asked whether I drink.

"Only to excess," I reply with a smile.

I'm only half-kidding. For whatever reason, I've never developed a taste for alcohol. Beer—yuck! I've had one in my life. To me, wine tastes like vinegar and hard alcohol like kerosene.

I do like mixed drinks like daiquiris or piña coladas, but that's only because the fruity flavors mask the taste of the alcohol.

In addition to the bad taste, alcohol is expensive and unhealthy.

For all of these reasons, I rarely drink.

But every few years, when I'm at a great party with friends, I'll drink a lot.

I've been really drunk fewer than a dozen times in my life. And, surprisingly, given how rarely I drink, I have only positive memories of these nights.

So I don't have a problem with anyone drinking—even occasionally to excess, as long as it's done safely.

But it's really important not to become a problem drinker or, worse yet, an alcoholic. Few things will destroy your life more thoroughly—it can even kill you. Over 72,000 Americans died from alcohol-related causes in 2017, up more than 100% in the past two decades and accounting for 2.6% of all deaths.

At a young age, I saw up close what alcoholism can do when I worked as a lifeguard for two summers at an alcoholic rehabilitation hospital in New Hampshire. Most of the "drunks," as they laughingly called themselves, had hit rock bottom, losing their jobs, marriages, etc.

Numerous studies support this anecdote. In the Harvard Study of Adult Development cited earlier, alcohol abuse was one of the major risk factors. Psychiatrist George Vaillant, who joined the team as a researcher in 1966 and led the study from 1972 until 2004, wrote that six factors predicted healthy aging for the Harvard men: physical activity, absence of alcohol abuse and smoking, having mature mechanisms to cope with life's ups and downs, a healthy weight, and a stable marriage.

In particular, he noted that "alcoholism and major depression could take people who started life as stars and leave them at the end of their lives as train wrecks." Alcoholism was the main cause of divorce among men in the study and was strongly correlated with neurosis and depression, which tended to follow alcohol abuse rather than precede it. Together with associated cigarette smoking, it was the single greatest contributor to early morbidity and death.

Even if you're not a problem drinker, much less an alcoholic, you must be careful about getting drunk because it can lead to disaster.

Let me tell you about a young guy I met years ago named

Genarlow Wilson. Raised by a single mom, he grew up poor outside Atlanta. Despite attending a number of tough schools, he was doing well in high school: he was an honor student, the star of the football team, homecoming king, and on his way to becoming the first person in his family to go to college.

But then, during his senior year, he got drunk at a party and received oral sex from a young woman from his high school. One of his classmates took a video of it, which ended up in the hands of the local district attorney, who charged Genarlow with aggravated child molestation, despite the fact the girl said it was consensual and there was only a two-year age difference between them (he was 17, she was 15). He refused to take a plea deal that would have required him to be labeled a child molester for life, so, under arcane state law, he was convicted and sentenced to ten years in adult state prison.

99% of the time, that would have been the end of the story. He would have been just one more young black man behind bars, his promising future over. But Genarlow got lucky— sort of. His sentence was so outrageous and so racist—this would have never happened to a white teenager—that a local lawyer took on the case pro bono and cleverly attracted a lot of media attention, including a *New York Times* editorial. After reading it, I reached out to her and ,at her request, I offered to post $1 million in bail. The Georgia Supreme Court ultimately ruled that Genarlow's sentence was cruel and unusual and ordered him released—but he had already served two years in prison.

A decade after that fateful night, Genarlow earned a degree in sociology from Morehouse College, and he is now married and a father—but he will never get back those two years. And it all started with getting drunk at a party.

It can be hard not to drink. All of us, especially young folks, will likely face pressure to join in. My oldest daughter, Alison, when she was a senior in high school, lost a number of friends because she didn't drink and therefore wasn't invited to their parties. That hurt her a lot—but I'm really proud of her for not succumbing to peer pressure.

In summary, I'm not telling you not to drink—nor even never to get drunk. But I am telling you to be careful where and with whom you get drunk and to stay far, far away from regular, heavy drinking.

DRUG ABUSE

I've never used drugs, not even once. The way I look at it, there are only two outcomes, and both are bad: either I will like it or I won't. If it feels great, then I'll probably want to do more of it and end up on the slippery slope to abuse and addiction. And if it makes me sick and miserable, why would I do it?

Even marijuana, which is now legal in many states, is very risky—a fact that a huge industry tries to hide. In fact, as journalist Alex Berenson argues in his powerful book, *Tell Your Children: The Truth About Marijuana, Mental Illness, and Violence*, if you discard the junk science, there's substantial evidence that marijuana is addictive, can lead some users to become terribly violent, and is linked to the development of schizophrenia, especially among young users. What sane person would want to play around with any of these risks?

As for harder drugs, more than 70,000 Americans died from overdoses in 2019—it's now the leading cause of death for people under 50. This chart shows the horrifying increase, driven by opioids[3]:

3   Kamp, Jon, and Campo-Flores, Arian. "The Opioid Crisis, Already Serious, Has Intensified During Coronavirus Pandemic" *The Wall Street Journal*, Sept. 2020, https://www.wsj.com/articles/the-opioid-crisis-already-serious-has-intensified-during-coronavirus-pandemic-11599557401.

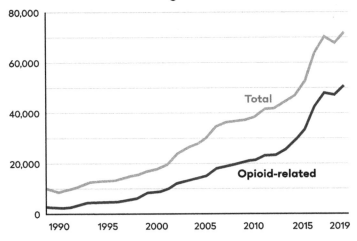

Number of Drug Deaths Per Year

Total

Opioid-related

Note: Numbers for 2019 are provisional and include projections.
Source: Centers for Disease Control and Prevention

I don't know what more I can say, other than to stay far, far away from drugs...

GAMBLING ADDICTION

I play a low-stakes game of poker with friends every month, co-chair a Texas hold 'em charity poker tournament every July, and occasionally enjoy an hour or two of blackjack at the $5 tables when I'm in Vegas. So, as with alcohol, I have no problem with a little bit of gambling. But, also as with alcohol, moderation is key because gambling can be addictive and, done to excess, life-destroying. A gambling problem can strain relationships, interfere with work, and cause people to run up huge debts or even steal money.

It's hard to draw a bright line between harmless and harmful gambling, but the North American Foundation for Gambling Addiction Help reports that approximately 2.6% of the US population has some type of gambling issue. That adds up to nearly 10 million people in the United States who struggle with a gambling habit.

It can take many forms—sports, scratch cards, roulette, poker, or slots—and take place in a casino, at the track, or online.

The most addictive casino game is the slot machine. Companies that design them hire psychologists to make them as addictive as possible. For example, if three triple-bars pay the big jackpot, the machine will show two triple-bars, and then, as the spinning slows, the third one is approaching...it's so close...will it get there? Aw, rats—it stopped just short! Of course, there was never any chance of winning the jackpot, but the machine is programmed to show frequent "near misses" to make the player think they were *this close* to winning. Studies have shown that slot machines can be as addictive as crack cocaine.

I saw this in the mid-1990s when I was running a nonprofit called The Initiative for a Competitive Inner City. We had a small office in Kansas City with an executive director, Larry, and his secretary, who liked to play the slots at the nearby riverboat casinos. Larry didn't have any idea that she was addicted until he discovered that she'd stolen $60,000 from the organization by falsifying his signature and bank statements for nearly a year. He fired her and reported her to the police, but the money was gone.

The most common form of gambling addiction I've seen is in the investment world. Over more than two decades in the business, I've seen how addictive trading stocks can be. People get hooked on the action of short-term trading, especially of highly risky and volatile stocks or, worse yet, options, and rapidly lose all of their money. The risk is especially great today with stocks soaring and easy-to-use trading platforms like Robinhood proliferating.

To make sure that I never fell into this deadly trap, when I was running my hedge fund, I never made any trades directly myself. Instead, I focused on making good investment decisions, and then, once I'd decided to, say, put on a 5% position in a particular stock, I'd email my broker to execute the order, thereby distancing myself from the trading.

SEX ADDICTION

I'm sure some people will read this and chuckle while thinking to themselves, "Pretty much every guy I know "suffers" from this "addiction." Indeed, considerable controversy surrounds the issue of sex addiction. It's been excluded from the fifth edition of the "Diagnostic and Statistical

Manual of Mental Disorders," but it's still written about and studied in psychology and counseling circles.

According to Health Online, sex addiction is "a compulsive need to perform sexual acts in order to achieve the kind of 'fix' that a person with alcohol use disorder gets from a drink or someone with opiate use disorder gets from using opiates. It shouldn't be confused with disorders such as pedophilia or bestiality."

For some people, sex addiction can be highly dangerous and result in considerable difficulties with relationships. Like drug or alcohol dependence, it has the potential to negatively impact a person's physical and mental health, personal relationships, quality of life, and safety.

Think of all the people like Tiger Woods who have been brought to absolute ruin because they couldn't keep their pants up. Sometimes their desire is rooted in power and misogyny; other times, they crave the adrenaline rush of seducing a new person.

If you're single, be careful! And if you're married, as I noted earlier, don't even flirt.

EATING DISORDERS

The single thing I worried about most as my daughters went

through their teenage years was that they might develop an eating disorder. It's a widespread problem in America. According to a 2018 *New York Times* article entitled "Recognizing Eating Disorders in Time to Help":

> "According to the Family Institute at Northwestern University, nearly 3% of teenagers between the ages of 13 and 18 have eating disorders. Boys as well as girls may be affected. Even when the disorder does not reach the level of a clinical diagnosis, some studies suggest that as many as half of teenage girls and 30% of boys have seriously distorted eating habits that can adversely affect them physically, academically, psychologically, and socially.
>
> Eating disorders can ultimately be fatal, said Dr. Laurie Hornberger, a specialist in adolescent medicine at Children's Mercy Kansas City. 'People with eating disorders can die of medical complications, but they may be even more likely to die of suicide. They become tired of having their lives controlled by eating and food issues.'
>
> The problem is especially common among, though not limited to, gymnasts, dancers, figure skaters, models, wrestlers, and other athletes, who often struggle to maintain ultra-slim bodies or maintain restrictive weight limits. The transgender population is also at higher risk for eating disorders.
>
> It is not unusual for teenagers to adopt strange or extreme

food-related behaviors, prompting many parents to think, 'This too shall pass.' But experts say an eating disorder—anorexia, bulimia or binge-eating—should not be considered 'normal' adolescent behavior, and they urge the adults in the youngsters' lives to be alert to telltale signs and take necessary action to stop the problem before it becomes entrenched."

As bad as the problem is nationally, it's an absolute epidemic among teenage girls in wealthy families like mine, thanks to a complicated web of factors, including a cultural emphasis on thinness and the systemic misogyny that led to it.

I can easily think of a half-dozen close friends with daughters who have eating disorders, and every time I go jogging in Central Park, I see multiple women who are clearly anorexic—just skin and bones (though almost half of those with anorexia are at or above normal weight). Eating disorders can last a lifetime and dramatically increase the chances of broken lives and, as noted above, even suicide. I've seen it up close, and it's heartbreaking.

The problem isn't limited to girls trying to lose weight. According to a 2019 study, "Predictors of muscularity-oriented disordered eating behaviors in US young adults," among young adults aged 18 to 24, 22% of males and 5% of females were striving to *gain* weight or build muscle by relying on risky eating habits, including overeating, and using poorly-tested dietary supplements and anabolic steroids.

On the other end of the spectrum, 60% of the girls surveyed said they were trying to lose weight. Some maintained unbalanced diets that can jeopardize growth and long-term health; others resorted to induced vomiting, laxatives, diuretics, diet pills, or engaged in other hazardous behaviors like fasting or excessive exercise.

The pandemic has undoubtedly made things worse, as this June 2020 op-ed in *The New York Times*, "Disordered Eating in a Disordered Time," highlights:

> "Then the pandemic happened and threw a huge wrench in my recovery," Mx. Roll said. 'The rationing of food, the loss of a regimented schedule. It all happened so quickly. It was the perfect ground for unhealthy coping mechanisms to start sucking me in.'

> Now Mx. Roll is not working, so the days are unstructured and lack the comfort of meals with neighbors. Mx. Roll feels anxious when friends report that, because of the pandemic, they are in the best shape of their lives. 'I keep having to remind myself that exercise and productivity don't define your worth,' Mx. Roll said.

> Roughly one in 10 Americans struggle with disordered eating, and the pandemic has created new hurdles for those managing difficult relationships with food. Working from home means spending the day next to a fully stocked refrigerator.

Grocery trips are less frequent, creating pressure to load up. Social meals are out of the question. And many individuals feel an enhanced degree of uncertainty and angst, which can exacerbate existing mental health challenges.

'When the world feels out of control, people want to have control over something,' said Jessica Gold, a psychiatrist at Washington University in St. Louis, who treats patients with eating and other mental health disorders. 'Often, it's what you put in your mouth.'

In March and April, the National Eating Disorders Association, or NEDA, saw a 78% increase in people messaging its helpline compared with the same period last year. Crisis Text Line, a nonprofit organization that provides mental health support by text, saw a 75% increase in conversations about eating disorders in the two months since March 16, to around 700 conversations from around 400 conversations weekly. A vast majority of those texters—83%—were women, and more than half were under the age of 17.

'There are jokes circulating about people's fear of weight gain during the pandemic,' said Claire Mysko, the chief executive officer of NEDA. 'There are influencers putting out messages about what you should and shouldn't be eating. On top of that we're seeing pictures of empty grocery shelves. That can be a trigger to people with eating disorders.'

Community is often a critical component of healing from an eating disorder, so the isolating nature of the pandemic has been especially difficult for those in recovery..."

In another *New York Times* article in May 2020, "I Have an Eating Disorder but Can't Escape the Kitchen," a woman named Susan Burton, who is in her mid-forties and has been struggling with eating disorders since adolescence, wrote:

"Stay-at-home orders present special challenges for people with eating disorders. The kitchen is always there: You can't get away from it. You can't get away from food online, either, where it's more present than ever: Sourdough starters and bean shortages and the ease with which people with healthier, typical relationships with food joke about these things, or fill their Instagrams with photos of family meals. I don't begrudge others that ease; I long for it.

Eating disorders are isolating. They are often misunderstood, perceived as the kind of thing you could get over if you just got a grip. Right now, many in our country are suffering profoundly, facing death and loss of livelihoods. Being able to afford food is a marker of privilege. Shouldn't our primary relationship with food be one of gratitude for it?

It's not that simple for people with eating disorders. For someone with an active eating disorder, food can be an agent of destruction. For someone in recovery, isolation can prompt a shift to old coping mechanisms..."

Parents need to be hypervigilant. If you suspect that your child has an eating disorder, intervene quickly and forcefully. It's critical to nip it in the bud—both before the disease progresses and before they turn 18 (at which point they are legally an adult, and you can no longer compel them to get treatment).

The Family Institute has listed these signs to look for:

- Restricting an increasing number of food groups without replacing them with others. "Kids announce they want to eat healthfully and eliminate sweets, then carbs, then fats, and soon there's little left."
- Significant weight change. Teenagers can become fixated on the numbers on the scale and continue to pursue weight loss despite having no evidence of a weight problem.
- Repeated extended trips to the bathroom, especially with water running to conceal vomiting, a part of the binge-and-purge cycle of bulimia.
- Excessive exercise, especially when coupled with restricted eating habits.
- Avoiding activities that involve food, like family meals or friends' parties. Comments like "I'll eat in my room" or "I'm not hungry—I had a big lunch" can be a sign of unhealthy food avoidance.

- When such indicators are coupled with accompanying symptoms like reduced energy, isolation, irritability, and social withdrawal, professional help should be sought. If possible, referral to an eating disorder center is ideal.

Susan and I very deliberately did a number of things to reduce the chances that our girls would develop eating disorders. We never discussed dieting or weight (studies show that dads are particularly important in this regard, so I was careful never to comment on *any woman's* appearance or weight).

I remember one time when I was out in the park with one of my friends and our daughters. We stopped at a convenience store to grab something to drink. When his 10-year-old selected a bottle of chocolate milk, he told her to put it back, saying, "That'll make you fat." I was horrified—he'd just dropped a neutron bomb on her, and wasn't even aware of it!

Susan and I have been careful never to make food an issue. She cooks healthy meals, and we have plenty of mostly healthy food in the house. But if the girls want to snack on Frosted Mini-Wheats or have a bowl of ice cream at night, we don't say a word.

And, as noted earlier, we raised them to be physically strong, athletic, and self-confident. While it's impossible to completely insulate them from outside pressure to look a certain way, all three of them are active and have healthy body images.

SPOUSAL ABUSE/DOMESTIC VIOLENCE

In the US, one in four women and one in seven men have been victims of severe physical violence (e.g., beating, burning, strangling) by an intimate partner in their lifetime. One in ten women has been raped by an intimate partner. Intimate partner violence accounts for 15% of all violent crimes.

Ideally, of course, you can detect anger management problems and/or a propensity for violence long before you get married—see question three of my 12 questions to ask before you marry someone. But if you find yourself married to someone who ever knowingly hurts you, get out fast! A few women in my extended family have been subjected to spousal abuse and, in every case, quickly divorced their husbands.

SEXUAL ABUSE

Sexual abuse of children is alarmingly common. One in nine girls and one in 53 boys under the age of eighteen experience sexual abuse or assault at the hands of an adult but only 16% of child victims tell someone about the abuse. And just 3% of sex offenders are caught and prosecuted.

There's been a lot of press regarding abuse by doctors, teachers, coaches, and religious leaders like priests, but it's actually twice as likely that the abuser is a family member, particularly a parent.

It's critical to keep a close eye on any situation in which adults spend unsupervised time with your children where "grooming" and then abuse can occur. Don't be paranoid, but also don't overlook warning signs. It is never normal for a 32-year-old to be best friends with a 12-year-old. If you ever detect inappropriate behavior, even one instance, you must expose and report it because—trust me—it's just the tip of the iceberg. *There is no such thing as someone who molests only one child.*

The risk doesn't end at age 18, of course. Depending on the survey, anywhere from 19% to 27% of women and 5% to 8% of men report being sexually assaulted in college. Thus, it's important to teach your college-bound children how to mitigate or avoid this risk.

Most college sex crimes occur when students have been drinking to excess—which, sadly, happens far too often. One survey revealed that 40% of college students had engaged in binge-drinking—five or more drinks within a two-hour period—in the previous two weeks. Young women need to be especially careful at frat parties and in other high-risk environments and during the first few months of their first and second semesters in college (more than 50% of college sexual assaults occur from August through November).

I've told my daughters many times that they're welcome to go to parties and have a drink or two—but they need to stay in control, so they're not targeted by a predator.

CALAMITY #5

THE DEATH, SERIOUS INJURY, OR ILLNESS OF YOURSELF OR A LOVED ONE

I've saved the biggest calamity for last. While deaths from illness, wars, crime, accidents, etc., have plunged over the centuries, millions of people still have their lives cut short or ruined by injury or illness, often in preventable ways.

In this chapter, I'd like to help you think about these risks, how to mitigate them, and how to think sensibly about which ones are worth taking.

MANAGING RISK DURING THE PANDEMIC

As I write this in January 2021, the coronavirus pandemic is at its worst point ever, with over 130,000 Americans hospitalized and more than 4,000 dying every day.

Vaccinations are ramping up rapidly, however, so by the time you read this, it may be mostly behind us and life will have returned to normal (I hope!)—if so, feel free to skip ahead.

Some argue that because fewer than 20% of Americans who have died of COVID-19 are under age 65—and most of these folks had comorbidities such as obesity, hypertension and/or diabetes—that young, reasonably healthy people don't need to worry about catching the virus because, even if they do, they likely won't have any symptoms, or, at worst, will simply have a few days of feeling like they have the flu.

This is bad thinking, and bad risk management, for two reasons: first, there are many cases in which young, healthy people suffer serious long-term consequences, such as extreme fatigue, loss of taste and/or smell, and even heart damage. While it's not known how common these outcomes are, there's clearly a "fat tail" risk that simply doesn't exist for, say, the common flu.

More importantly, young people with the virus (especially asymptomatic ones who don't know they have it) can spread it—which keeps the pandemic raging—and ultimately infect vulnerable people, many of whom become sick, have to be hospitalized, and even die.

So, no matter what your age and health, you should treat the virus very seriously and do your best to avoid getting (and spreading) it.

To do so, start by following the basic measures espoused by Dr. Fauci and the CDC: wear a mask, maintain social distancing, avoid crowds and poorly ventilated spaces, and wash your hands often.

These recommendations are obvious and, for most people, fairly easy to implement. I'm still able to meet up with friends, go jogging, and play tennis, for example—I just do all of these activities outdoors.

Unfortunately, however, the response to the pandemic has been politicized, which has led tens of millions of Americans to believe that it's nothing to worry about, and/or a hoax, and/or that wearing a mask is an unacceptable infringement on their freedom. This is madness!

Worse yet, tens of millions of Americans (likely many of the same folks) aren't planning to get vaccinated when it becomes available. According to Gallup's latest polling, 35% of Americans say they'd refuse an FDA-approved vaccine, even if it were offered at no cost. And, sadly, there's a huge partisan split: only 17% of Democrats vs. 55% of Republicans would say no. I sure hope these surveys are wrong, because it would be a national tragedy if this terrible pandemic is prolonged by many months, accompanied by hundreds of thousands of incremental, unnecessary deaths, due to false information and conspiracy theories leading many folks to eschew a vaccination.

Even if you have the good sense to follow the basics, however, there are still a lot of tough decisions everyone has to make pretty much every day. For example, should you take a ride in a friend's car? Outdoor tennis is probably safe, but what about indoors? Do you spend a holiday with your parents? The list of tricky questions is endless.

There are no blanket answers to these questions, as every person has a different risk tolerance, personal situation (age, health, do you interact with vulnerable people?), and environment (is there a flare-up in your area?).

I tend to have a pretty high tolerance for risk, plus I don't have many risk factors: I'm not old yet (I'm 54), am in superb health, and, living on the Upper East Side of Manhattan, have access to the best doctors in the world. Thus, I've been willing to take risks that I wouldn't recommend to others, such as flying out West to go rock climbing last June and October and taking my family to Kenya to spend three weeks with my parents and sister over the recent Christmas holidays.

There is one area, however, in which I've recently changed

my mind—and behavior. I'm a passionate pickup basketball player. Pre-pandemic, I'd been playing 2-3 times a week for decades with a group of friends. That all came to full stop last spring when the pandemic walloped New York City.

But then the number of cases, hospitalizations, and deaths here plunged by more than 90%, so in the fall, my friends and I played basketball a few times outdoors in Central Park. And then, in November and December, a dozen of us rented a gym and played for a couple of hours on Sunday nights.

This was probably the highest-risk thing I'd done since the start of the pandemic: it was indoors, we were all sweating and breathing hard, and were right in each other's faces playing defense—with no masks. I decided to take the risk because the virus was at such low levels in New York City.

However, when I came back from Kenya this month and the Sunday night games resumed, the environment had changed dramatically: cases, hospitalizations, deaths, and the percentage of people testing positive had soared to six to ten times above the levels at the beginning of November! Thus, even though I'd already paid for eight Sundays in January, February, and March, I decided to sit out until we all got vaccinated or the COVID numbers fell a lot.

This example underscores a key principle of risk management: it's not enough to identify risks and take steps to mitigate them on a one-time basis upfront. It's also important to monitor changing risk levels and, if necessary, make adjustments.

TOP 10 CAUSES OF DEATH IN THE UNITED STATES

75% of all deaths in the United States are attributable to the following ten causes, listed in descending order (this list excludes 2020 when COVID-19 was #3):

- Heart disease
- Cancer
- Accidents
- Chronic lower respiratory disease (often caused by smoking)
- Stroke and cerebrovascular diseases
- Alzheimer's disease
- Diabetes
- Influenza and pneumonia
- Kidney disease
- Suicide

The top three account for 50% of all deaths. Many of these deaths are preventable, particularly for younger people. In fact, the leading cause of death for Americans between the ages of one and 44 is an accident.

DEADLY DISEASES LIKE CANCER

Let's start with deadly diseases, which account for eight of the top 10 causes of death.

I have two general pieces of advice here: first, try to reduce the chances that you get one of these diseases; and second, take steps to detect them early so you'll have a much better chance of surviving them.

Regarding the former, sometimes people with no risk factors whatsoever nevertheless contract a deadly disease. There's a random element that's frightening. For example, my uncle developed dementia and rapidly deteriorated to his current vegetative state.

But, let's be honest, many diseases are the direct result of certain behaviors—for example, a smoker getting lung cancer. So, first and foremost, don't use any tobacco products. Don't smoke, chew tobacco, or puff on e-cigarettes.

If you're currently a smoker, don't say to yourself, "What's the point of quitting now? The damage has already been done, so it's too late..." This is emphatically not true—studies show large, immediate health benefits irrespective of when you quit.

Many of the other diseases are related to diet and fitness. People with an unhealthy diet who rarely exercise and/or are overweight are far more likely to have heart disease or diabetes, suffer a stroke, etc. I share some tips for taking better care of your body at the end of this chapter.

The other key to combatting diseases is getting proper screening. My cousin put off getting a mammogram for years because she was busy. Since she had no family history of breast cancer, she didn't worry about it. But when she finally had one, doctors discovered an aggressive form of breast cancer. Fortunately, it was at an early stage, so she only had to do radiation therapy, not chemotherapy or surgery. As of this writing, she appears to have beaten the cancer, but her doctors told her that if she had waited any longer to get screened, it likely would have been fatal.

Colon cancer is the second leading cancer killer (after lung cancer). Caught in the first or second stage, nine out of ten people will survive at least five years. But if it's not caught until stage four, only 10% of people survive five years.

Early screening is the best way to mitigate the risk, but many people put it off.

Consequently, 60% of colon cancers are detected in a late stage.

The primary reason people don't get a colonoscopy when they should is that it's unpleasant. You have to drink a massive amount of nasty-tasting liquid that induces diarrhea to clean out your system. Then you have to go to a hospital or clinic and get knocked out with anesthesia before they put a scope with a camera up your butt. Not surprisingly, many people (especially men) feel squeamish about it.

The result, however, is that most people who get colon cancer don't realize there's a problem until they see blood in their stool. At that point, it's generally in stage four, and little can be done.

So get a colonoscopy when you turn 50! I can say from experience that it's no fun, but it's worth it. During my first colonoscopy a few years ago, they found and removed a precancerous polyp, which means I need to go back for another one in five years, not 10.

ACCIDENTS

Let's start with some good news: over the past century, Americans have become 96% less likely to be killed in an automobile accident, 88% less likely to be struck and killed as pedestrians, 99% less likely to die in a plane crash, 59% less likely to fall to their deaths, 92% less likely to die by fire, 90% less likely to drown, 92% less likely to be asphyxiated and 95% less likely to be killed on the job.

That said, there are 170,000 fatal accidents every year in

the United States, 75% of which occur in the home. The five most common are, in order (with tips to mitigate them):

- Poisoning (mostly overdoses and carbon monoxide)
    - Buy a carbon monoxide detector.
    - Keep poisons like household cleaners, alcohol, and medications locked up.
    - Use sensors with sirens on the liquor cabinet and medicine cabinet.
    - Don't reuse milk or juice cartons for other purposes.
    - Educate your children about the safety hazards of household cleaners, drugs, and alcohol.
- Falling
    - Use safety gates on stairs to keep babies and toddlers safe.
    - Use rug pads to avoid tripping hazards.
    - Use grab bars in the bathroom.
    - Use night-lights in hallways and on stairs.
    - Add treads to slippery stairs.
- Choking/suffocation (the leading cause of accidental deaths for infants)
    - For babies and younger kids, cut up food into small bites.
    - Supervise young kids when they're eating.
    - Secure power cords and blinds cords to avoid strangulation hazards.
    - Keep pillows, blankets, and soft toys out of baby cribs.

- Drowning
  - Never leave a child unattended around water, including bathtubs, pools, lakes, streams, etc.
  - Add gate sensors to pool areas.
  - Use water sensors in pool areas to alert you to an unexpected splash.
  - Use proper water safety equipment like life preservers whenever on a boat, fishing, etc.
- Fires/burns
  - Don't leave candles or fireplaces unattended.
  - Regularly test smoke alarms and change the batteries every six months.
  - Don't leave food or kettles on the stove unattended.
  - Use safety gates around fireplaces and barbecues if there are little ones around.

CAR CRASHES

38,800 Americans died in car accidents in 2019. With all the new safety features in cars, you might think that the numbers would be declining, but fatalities per mile driven only declined 4% in the past two years, after rising 13% in the prior two years.

This risk factor is very personal to me because, while I can't recall even one serious car accident involving me or anyone I know in the first 50 years of my life, in the past three years, my wife, three cousins, and three friends have been in seven—SEVEN!—serious accidents. In each case, their cars were totaled, resulting in multiple concussions and, tragically, two deaths. This has affected me deeply and led me to do a lot of research on car safety.

Let's start with the obvious: wear your seat belt! The 13% of Americans who don't wear seat belts account for *half* of auto fatalities.

Equally obvious: don't drink and drive. Drunk driving causes more than 10,000 deaths in the US every year—nearly one-third of the traffic-related total and more than one every hour. Even a drink or two is dangerous: at a blood alcohol concentration of 0.05—roughly two drinks, at which point it's still legal to drive in all 50 states—you've *doubled* your odds of a traffic accident. At 0.08 (three to four drinks), the legal limit in most states, your odds have *quadrupled*.

If you've had too much to drink, have a friend drive you home or take a taxi or Uber—don't walk. Drunk walking is five times more dangerous than drunk driving (per mile) because tipsy people tend to wander into the road.

Don't rush. The single biggest cause of fatal accidents is speeding. Does it really matter if you get somewhere a few minutes later? I used to be a chronic speeder, but now I set the adaptive cruise control to five to ten mph over the speed limit, relax, and enjoy listening to the radio or an Audible book.

Beware of distracted driving. There's always been the distraction of phone calls, but now it's much worse with drivers messing around with Google Maps, Spotify, text messages, and every type of social media. More than ever, drivers are taking their eyes off the road—and the consequences can be deadly.

Most importantly, don't allow yourself to get distracted. But what about other drivers who might slam into you? My advice here is: if you can afford it, get a late-model car with the latest safety features.

A few years ago, as part of some investment research, I began studying the safety features that are increasingly standard in new cars, and I was amazed. There are so many features that can both help you avoid accidents and, if you're in one, mitigate injuries.

After learning more, I decided to trade in our 10-year-old Volvo XC90 in 2016 and upgrade to a brand-new 2017 model. It proved to be a wise decision.

A week after buying our new car, Susan and I were driving from New York to Maine to visit our daughter at camp. While cruising along around sixty mph in heavy traffic near Boston, a car far ahead of us suddenly braked, causing a chain reaction. Before we knew it, we were about to rear-end the car ahead of us. But then the frontal collision-avoidance system kicked in: an alarm went off, a red image flashed on the windshield, the car automatically jammed on the brakes, and we stopped in the nick of time.

A year later, the new safety features could have literally been a lifesaver. We were spending Thanksgiving at my in-laws' house in western Massachusetts. Alison had a flight out of Hartford at six in the morning, so Susan woke up at four and drove her to the airport. She hadn't had much sleep, and on the way back, she struggled to stay awake. Only five minutes from returning safely, she fell asleep behind the wheel and, when the road curved, went straight ahead.

Though it was a wooded area, she got incredibly lucky and went into a field. The car hit a stump, shearing off the front-left wheel, and continued for another hundred yards, coming to rest between two trees. Here's a picture of it:

Every airbag deployed, but the body of the car was intact. Susan was badly shaken but completely uninjured.

Before the car even came to a stop, the Volvo On-Call phone system had called emergency services. Within a few seconds, the operator came on: "We have a report that your airbag has deployed. Are you okay?"

"Yes, I'm okay," Susan replied.

"Would you like us to call the police for you?" the operator asked.

"Yes, please," she replied.

"Would you like us to stay on the phone until someone arrives?"

"Yes, please."

Police arrived in two minutes.

Susan was very lucky. She was on a back road and wasn't driving fast. She didn't drift into oncoming traffic. She didn't flip the car, hit a tree, or go down a ravine. And she was driving one of the safest cars in the world.

There are a few takeaways from this accident. First, don't

drive when you're tired. You're in control of a two-ton metal missile moving at high speed. Pull over and take a break. Drink some coffee or Coke (you might even consider keeping caffeine pills in the glove compartment). When you get back on the road, roll down the window, blast loud music, or call a friend. A friend of mine once pushed the Volvo On-Call button and spoke to the operator to stay awake on a long drive in the middle of the night.

Second, if you're driving a car that's more than five years old and can afford to replace it with a new one, do so! And if you can't afford a new one now, when you do buy one, either new or used, look for key safety features.

Also, don't give the old family car to your child who is just learning to drive or going off to college. If it's not safe enough for you, why would it be safe enough for your child? When Alison needed a car for her summer job in 2017, we didn't even consider buying a used one. Instead, we bought a new Subaru Outback, which, fully loaded, cost around $35,000. Subarus last forever, are a lot cheaper than Volvos, and are nearly as safe.

Lastly, when renting a car, I used to always get the economy-sized one, but now I make sure to rent at least a full-size car. The odds of an accident are much higher when you're driving an unfamiliar car in an unfamiliar city, so at least make sure the car is safe.

MOTORCYCLES

I've ridden motorcycles a few times and love the thrill of feeling their power and speed. But they're incredibly dangerous. Per mile traveled, motorcyclists are *16 times* more likely to get injured and *35 times* more likely to be killed than someone in a car. 80% of motorcycle crashes result in injury or death, compared to only 20% of car crashes.

My friend Guy Spier used to ride a high-powered BMW motorcycle, but after his first child was born, he got rid of it. He correctly recognized that it was no longer a risk worth taking.

If you choose to ride a motorcycle, at least make sure you wear a helmet at all times (which goes for any high-speed activity, such as biking, skiing, snowboarding, or horseback riding.)

SANE VS. INSANE RISKS

I love an adventure and am willing to take risks to have one. But there's a difference between sane and insane risks. In the former category, in my opinion, are rock climbing roped to a professional guide (for example, in June 2020, I climbed The Nose of El Capitan in Yosemite National Park), parachuting strapped to an instructor, and bungee jumping. Yes, there's some risk, but if you're doing the activity right, it's minimal.

In the insane category are things like free soloing (what Alex Honnold did in the movie, *Free Solo*, climbing El Capitan without a rope), BASE jumping, wingsuit flying, and flying ultralight aircraft (which killed my friend, Walmart heir John Walton in 2005). No matter how good you are, the inherent risk of these activities is extreme, and an alarming percentage of participants end up dead.

Somewhere in the middle are climbing high-altitude mountains like Denali or Everest, flying gliders (which my father and sister do in Kenya), hang gliding, and paragliding. I went paragliding while strapped to a professional at the Jackson Hole ski area in the summer of 2008, and it was great fun. But my dad almost died doing it.

He lived in Ethiopia at the time, where he lived for eight years before moving to Kenya. One day, he drove to a remote area far outside the capital, hiked to the top of a hill, and took off. He was soaring beautifully when a mini-tornado of some sort collapsed his wing. It wasn't a freefall, but he spiraled down 75 feet onto some rocks.

Thankfully, when he'd bought his harness system, he'd paid extra for one with a built-in airbag. He writes: "Clearly, it saved my life and even kept my spine from breaking. The company that made the airbag commented that they had never seen one exploded like mine was."

Still, he broke his wrist and was bleeding internally, so he was in quite a bit of pain during the half-hour walk back to his car and hour-long drive to a hospital.

My mom freaked out when he started to urinate blood, so they quickly booked a flight to Nairobi, where the hospitals and doctors are better. (His medivac insurance company refused to pay for an air ambulance plane because he was engaged in a "hazardous sport.")

He ended up recovering well but needed a couple of surgeries on his wrist—and, needless to say, has never paraglided again.

This is a good example of how some activities, done wisely, are sane, but done recklessly, are insane. My dad was doing something that, while inherently dangerous, wasn't likely to be deadly—but then he layered on multiple additional risks: he was alone, fairly inexperienced, didn't know the area (or its winds), was far from a hospital and, to top it off, was in one of the poorest countries in the world with an inferior medical system. He's lucky he didn't pay for these mistakes with his life.

TAKING SMART RISKS AND INVESTING IN SAFETY

While I do plenty of risky things, I'm very conscious about the level of risk and think carefully about how to reduce it.

BIKING

By far, the single most dangerous thing I do is ride my bike almost every day on the streets of Manhattan, come rain, snow, or shine. I like the exercise, it's a fast way to get around, and I'm never late because I know, to the minute, exactly how long it will take me to get to my destination since there's no chance of getting stuck in traffic or on the subway.

But it's risky. While there have been some improvements like bike lanes on a few streets, Manhattan isn't a bike-friendly place. I'm always dodging pedestrians, cars, trucks, and buses—and one mistake can be fatal.

This really hit home when my daughters' pediatrician (for a decade when they were younger) was riding across Central Park on the narrow, two-way road on 97th Street last December. It was only a half-mile from his apartment to his office, but he slipped on a patch of ice and fell under the wheel of a school bus, killing him instantly.

The risk isn't high enough to scare me off my bike, but it's led me to take a number of steps:

- I invested in a bike with disk brakes (and keep it well maintained), so I can stop on a dime, even when it's wet.
- I spent $150 on two super-bright blinking lights, one on my front handlebar and the other on my seat stem, facing backward.

- I invested another $200 in a Lumos helmet, which has a series of super-bright blinking lights embedded in the front and back of the helmet. In addition, if it detects me braking suddenly, two more big red lights in the back light up to warn vehicles behind me—just like when you hit the brakes of your car. With all of these lights blinking madly, day and night, I look like a Christmas tree, but they make me much more visible to both vehicles and pedestrians, which I'm convinced has saved me from collisions on more than one occasion.

- I can't say I always stop at red lights or stop signs, but I always slow down when approaching an intersection and look both ways to ensure I don't hit any pedestrians or get hit by a car coming from the cross street.

- I generally won't bike farther south than 40th Street (about two and a half miles from my apartment on 98th Street) because the streets get more narrow, crowded, and unfamiliar. If I have to go farther south, I take the subway instead.

CLIMBING

In the summer of 2015, Susan and I did the famous Haute Route, a week-long, hut-to-hut glacier trek from Chamonix, France, at the base of Mont Blanc, the highest peak in the Alps, to Zermatt, Switzerland, at the base of one of the world's most iconic peaks, the Matterhorn. We discovered that we both love trekking and climbing in the mountains, enjoying the spectacular beauty of the great outdoors and the physical and mental challenges. But unlike Susan, when I looked up at Mont Blanc and the Matterhorn, I had a burning desire to climb them, so I vowed to come back the next year and try.

Before doing so, however, I did some research on how dangerous they are. I learned that a handful of people die on these peaks every year—roughly one of every 5,000 people who attempt Mont Blanc and one in 2,000 on the hairier Matterhorn. I didn't like those odds, but when I dug deeper, it turned out that most deaths occurred among inexperienced amateurs climbing without guides. In fact, I coulnd't find a single story about someone dying while roped to a professional guide.

So I decided to do two things: 1) get training; and 2) hire Geoffroy Arvis, one of the two professionals who'd guided Susan and me (and five others) on the Haute Route.

To learn the basics of rock climbing and mountaineering, I signed up for a five-day private training course at a mountaineering school called Petra Cliffs in Burlington, Vermont. The husband-and-wife team who run it, Steve and Andrea Charest, took me into the White Mountains and gave me a crash course on equipment, knots, lead climbing, and many other skills.

Then, when I actually did the climbs, I was roped to Geoffroy at every moment, which certainly aligned our interests! He is one of only roughly 6,000 people to be certified by the International Federation of Mountain Guides Associations. These guys (almost all are men) are superstars. They go through a rigorous, multiyear training program, so they are superior climbers and skiers, know the mountains, understand weather patterns, and can identify hidden dangers like crevasses and avalanche zones.

A guide's job is not only to keep you safe *on* the mountain but perhaps even more importantly, to keep you *off* the mountain if snow or weather conditions are dangerous. For example, I met Geoffroy in Chamonix on July 1, 2017, for our planned ascent of Mont Blanc the next day. But on the morning of the 2nd, he looked at the forecast and didn't like what he saw—showers and thunderstorms in the afternoon—so he delayed us by a day.

Had I been on my own, I probably would have risked it because I was on a tight schedule. The plan called for us to summit and then descend Mont Blanc on July 3rd, drive to Zermatt on the morning of the 4th, and hike up to the hut at the base of the Matterhorn that afternoon. Then, we'd summit on the morning of the 5th, and I'd take a train back to Geneva that afternoon to catch my flight home the next morning.

By delaying us by a day, Geoffroy killed my plans to climb the Matterhorn on this trip—I ended up having to fly back to Europe to climb it a month later—but that wasn't his concern. He was too wise and experienced to take any chances with thunderstorms.

Sure enough, soon thereafter, an American woman was killed by a lightning strike near the summit of the Matterhorn. Her mistake was still being on the mountain in the late afternoon when storms tend to come in. In contrast, when I climbed both Mont Blanc and the Matterhorn, Geoffroy had us out of the hut at 4 a.m., on the summit by 9 a.m., and back in the hut, enjoying lunch by 1 p.m.

Lastly, Geoffroy kept me safe when we were climbing. I can't imagine doing either of these climbs without a seasoned guide. Though the routes were well-trafficked, there were many times when I could have gotten off the trail—which can be deadly. There are dozens of places where one slip can lead to a fatal fall.

After hearing about my climbs in the Alps and, more recently, Yosemite, people often ask me if my next goal is to climb Mount Everest. My answer is always, "Absolutely not." The highest peak in the Alps, Mont Blanc, is only 15,781 feet, well below Everest's 29,029. In the Alps, there's no "death zone," whereas, near the top of Everest, the air is so thin you can only survive for a few hours without supplemental oxygen. 8% of climbers who have attempted Everest have died. It's much lower if you exclude those who climbed without oxygen or guides, but it's still an unacceptable level of risk for me.

MITIGATING OTHER RISKS

Anyone who does backcountry hiking or skiing during the winter has to think carefully about the risk of an avalanche. I know nothing about avalanches, so I always go with a guide or experienced friend and wear a backpack with an inflatable balloon, a relatively new safety device that helps someone caught in an avalanche ride on top of it so that, when it ends, they are less likely to be buried and suffocate.

Another risk I've taken is having two types of eye surgery on my eyes: first, two decades ago, I had LASIK to correct my distance vision. Then, a couple of years ago, I had a KAMRA inlay in one eye to correct my close-up vision, so I almost never need reading glasses.

In both cases, I carefully researched the procedures and risks. Once I decided to have them done, I didn't go with the cheapest option (neither was covered by insurance, so I had to pay out of pocket). Instead, I found the most experienced doctors with a history of success in these surgeries. In the case of LASIK, when I had it done, it was still a relatively new procedure in the US but had been approved years earlier in Canada, so I flew to Toronto to have it done with a doctor who'd done it more than 10,000 times.

Lastly, despite all of my efforts to mitigate risk, I know there are no guarantees, so years ago, I bought a $10 million life insurance policy to make sure my family is taken care of if I bite the big one. I love joking with people who ask what Susan thinks of my various high-risk endeavors by replying, "Well, ever since I got a $10 million life insurance policy, she hasn't expressed any worries whatsoever!"

SUICIDE

In 2018, there were 48,344 recorded suicides in the US, making it the tenth most common cause of death—and it's rising. After bottoming out in 1999, the age-adjusted suicide rate in the US increased by 24% by 2016, reaching the highest rate recorded in 28 years, as you can see in this chart:[4]

---

4   https://en.wikipedia.org/wiki/Suicide_in_the_United_States.

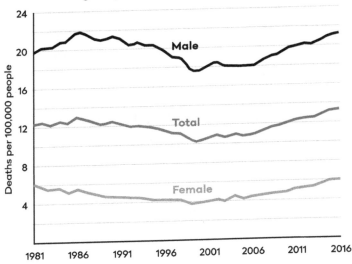

Age-Adjusted US Suicide Rate, 1986–2016

Deaths per 100,000 people

Male

Total

Female

If you are a parent of a teenager or young adult, you need to think especially hard about this risk, as suicide is the third and second most common cause of death for Americans between the ages of 10-14 and 15-34, respectively.

In particular, suicide has skyrocketed among teenage girls: up 151% for younger teens and 77% for older teen girls from the average of 2000-2009 to 2017. Additionally, hospital admissions due to self-harm are up 189% for 10-14-year-old girls and 52% for 15-19-year-old girls since 2009.

Experts aren't sure why, but I think NYU Marketing Professor Scott Galloway nails it when he writes:

"There are many factors, but ground zero is the nuclear weapons [smartphones with Facebook and other social media] we've put in girls' hands to objectify them, perpetually undercut their self-esteem, and enable them to bully each other relationally, 24/7."

If you have even the slightest hint that someone you love might be suicidal, *take action*! For starters, call the National Suicide Prevention Lifeline at 800-273-8255. Then, find a good psychiatrist or counselor and try to get the person to see him or her. There are many therapies and medications that can make a huge difference.

GUNS

I could have put this section under accidents, but instead, put it here because guns are used in almost half of all suicides in the US.

Before diving in, I want to be clear that I don't question the *right* of law-abiding citizens to have a gun—I just, in most cases, question their *wisdom*.

The combination of the coronavirus and the George Floyd/ Black Lives Matter/Defund the Police movements have led to a surge in people buying guns. Background checks ,which tend to closely track actual sales, were up 60% year over year in 2020.

Most people have a gun for safety—to protect themselves—yet ironically, it's the single thing in their home most likely to harm them or a loved one.

Gun accidents are alarmingly common. Think of the young man who comes home late and is shot by his father, who thought he was an intruder. Or the guy who shoots his friend or wife in a burst of rage (the presence of a gun in a domestic violence situation increases the risk of homicide *six-fold*). Or the child who plays with a gun and it goes off (tragically, children aged five to eleven are 11 *times* more likely to be fatally shot in the United States than in any other developed country).

I've seen how easily it can happen. In high school, I almost shot my best friend with a shotgun while hunting. I was walking in the lead, and he was 30 feet behind me. Suddenly, a pheasant burst out of the brush behind us, and we both turned at the same time and shot. He brought down the bird. I, on the other hand, saw my buckshot whiz only inches above the top of his head (I didn't tell him for 20 years)!

But the biggest risk of having a gun in your house isn't an accident—it's suicide. There's a lot of (well-deserved) press around guns being used to murder people, but 60% of gun deaths in 2017 were from suicide, not homicide.

Overall, gun owners are nearly *four times* as likely to die by suicide than people without guns, even when controlling for gender, age, race, and neighborhood.

The risk is particularly high for first-time gun buyers. A recent study tracked nearly 700,000 first-time handgun buyers in California, year by year, and compared them with similar nonowners, measuring risk by gender. Men who bought a gun for the first time were *eight times* as likely to kill themselves by gunshot in the subsequent 12 years than nonowners; women were *35 times* as likely to do so.

Speaking of gender differences, 16% of men who attempt suicide succeed, but only 3% of women do because men are far more likely to use a gun, which is fatal 82.5% of the time. Women, in contrast, are most likely to take pills/poison, which is fatal only 1.5% of the time.

Those who doubt that it matters—"If the first attempt fails, they'll just do it later"—couldn't be more wrong. In fact, of the 91% of people who survive their first suicide attempt, 70% never try again, and only 7% later succeed.

This is because, contrary to popular perception, most suicide attempts are impulsive, prompted by a fleeting crisis, depression, drunkenness (33%), or drugs (24%). Thus, it's critical that there isn't a gun nearby when the impulse strikes.

To understand how important it is to keep guns out of homes, consider this: the suicide *attempt* rate in South Carolina is 28% higher than in Maryland, yet the suicide *death* rate is 67% higher. Why? More homes with guns.

In summary, if you own a gun, I strongly urge you to think long and hard about the risk you're taking. Do you really need it? Unless you live in a high-crime neighborhood, you'll probably never use it to protect yourself.

If you feel that you must own a gun, at least get a big one—handguns are used in 69% of firearm suicides (65% for males, 88% for females). And make it difficult to access. Keep the unloaded gun separate from the ammunition, which should be under lock and key (and don't tell anyone in the family where the key is). If you use it for hunting, can you keep it somewhere out of your home?

HAVING YOUR BODY BREAK DOWN

While, of course, not as serious as dying, having your body break down prematurely is a genuine calamity. Most people don't take care of their bodies—more than two-thirds of Americans are overweight, and 40% are obese. As a result, as they age, they often suffer years of pain and disability and die years before they should.

Buffett gives a wonderful analogy: "If you were only given

one car and you had to make it last for your entire life, imagine how you'd treat it: you'd drive it slowly and carefully, change the oil regularly, etc."

Yet most people do the opposite with their bodies: they stuff it full of sugar and fat, poison it with drugs, cigarettes, and excess amounts of alcohol, and do little to no exercise.

If you take nothing else from this book, vow to treat your body better. You don't have to be perfect—everyone has their vices (mine are Diet Coke, candy, and a little ice cream sundae every night)—but you can go far by taking a lot of small steps over time.

NUTRITION

I don't follow any particular diet, nor am I a nutritionist. I just try to eat mostly healthy foods and avoid overeating.

Rather than trying to change everything at once, you might think about giving up (or at least cutting back on) something you know isn't good for you.

For thirty years, I ate a lot of candy every day—I had huge five-pound bags of gummy bears and Twizzlers in my cabinet, from which I would refill a little bag I kept with me at all times. I ate it very slowly, but the near-constant infusion of sugar added up.

Then I went on a trip to Europe a few summers ago and didn't take any candy with me. I found that I didn't miss it, so when I returned, I threw away all of my candy and never looked back. I quickly lost 10 pounds—and my teeth and stomach thank me every day! I didn't give up candy entirely—for example, I'll chew on some to help me concentrate on a long drive—but I'd estimate that I've reduced my consumption by more than 90%.

A healthy diet isn't just what you eat, but how much. Portion sizes today are so much larger than in the past that it encourages overeating. To combat this, when I eat out, I deliberately order something that's good reheated—pasta rather than a burger and fries, for example—and then I bring half of the meal home. It drives Susan crazy sometimes because our refrigerator can get filled with leftovers that we end up throwing out, but it's better than overeating!

EXERCISE

Countless studies show that regular exercise leads to better health and fitness, a lower risk of many diseases, and a longer life expectancy. It literally reshapes aging. In various recent studies, active older people's muscles, immune systems, blood cells, and even skin appeared biologically younger, at a molecular level, than those of sedentary people.

Exercise also leads to more energy and self-confidence,

lower stress, better sleep, and more happiness. Physically active people are half as likely to be depressed.

But wait, there's more: studies show that exercise increases your memory, learning, creativity, productivity, and self-control. Many people who begin to exercise stop using their credit cards so often. They procrastinate less at work. They do the dishes earlier in the day.

An article in *The New York Times* summarizes:

> "Scientists have found and reaffirmed the extent to which movement, of almost any kind and amount, may remake how we think and feel. In one study after another, physical activity beneficially remodeled the brains of children and the middle-aged; lowered people's risks for dementia or, if dementia had already begun, slowed memory loss; and increased brain volume, tissue health, and the quality of connections between neurons and different portions of the brain.
>
> Exercise also seems able to buoy moods far more than most of us, including scientists, might have expected 10 years ago. In observational studies, physically active people proved to be much less likely to develop depression or anxiety than sedentary people, no matter what types of activities they chose."

So get into the habit of regular exercise by finding something you enjoy. I like to mix it up: pickup basketball one day, going to the gym the next, then tennis the next, maybe a good run or race on the weekend. Plus, I ride my bike around the city pretty much every day. At least twice a week, I try to mix in high-intensity interval training, which studies show is important—usually via a session with a personal trainer or running coach or a boutique fitness class like Tone House.

Susan, in contrast, is a creature of habit: she gets up early every morning and does the exact same workout on an elliptical machine in the gym in the basement of our building.

Figure out what works for you—but make it a habit! If I go more than a day without a good workout, I really notice it. I know we're all super busy, but even if you're short on time, you'd be amazed at how much of a sweat you can work up in only a few minutes—for example, I sometimes use the *7 Minute Workout* app.

Dr. Yoni Freedhoff, an Associate Professor of Family Medicine at the University of Ottawa, shared this advice in an op-ed published in *The New York Times*:

> "After practicing family medicine for 16 years, with a focus on nutrition and obesity, I've learned that the keys to good health are quite simple to describe. In fact, I believe the best health advice can be boiled down to 48 words:

Don't smoke.

Get vaccinated.

Avoid trans fats.

Replace saturated fats with unsaturated if you can.

Cook from whole ingredients—and minimize restaurant meals.

Minimize ultraprocessed foods.

Cultivate relationships.

Nurture sleep.

Drink alcohol at most moderately.

Exercise as often as you can enjoy.

Drink only the calories you love."

===

SNIPPETS OF ADVICE FOR GROWTH AND SUCCESS IN BUSINESS AND IN LIFE

This book so far has focused on avoiding calamities—in other words, playing defense. Now, I'd like to end the book by talking about playing offense.

DEVELOP GOOD HABITS

You can transform yourself into the person you want to be, but you have to decide early because the chains of habit are too light to be felt until they are too heavy to be broken.

—WARREN BUFFETT

Think about that. All the little things you do dozens of times every day—your habits—define who you are, and once these patterns are set, they're really tough to change. Thus, it's critically important to develop good habits early in life.

Buffett tells students to look at the people you work or go to school with and ponder this question: "Who do you think is going to be really successful in life, not just financially, but in every way?

As you think about this, what are the characteristics you're focusing on? Are they smart? Do they work really hard and not give up easily? Do they have integrity? Is their word their bond? Are they 100% reliable? Are they well organized? Do they take care of themselves and not take foolish risks? Are they kind and a pleasure to spend time with? Do they make the world a better place?

Now ask yourself: what are they doing that I can't do as well? I think you'll find at least 90% of these traits are things over which you have total control.

So you see, you don't need me to tell you what habits you should try to adopt—you already know. There's no secret—they're obvious! The real question is: what are you going to do about it?"

INTEGRITY, INTELLIGENCE, AND ENERGY

Turning to Buffett again:

> "Somebody once said that in looking for people to hire, you look for three qualities: integrity, intelligence, and energy. And if you don't have the first, the other two will kill you. You think about it; it's true. If you hire somebody without [integrity], you really want them to be dumb and lazy."

In this chapter, I'll discuss all three of the qualities Buffett mentions: integrity, intelligence, and energy.

By "energy," Buffett's not just talking about putting in a lot of hours—though that's part of it—but also maximizing the value of those hours by being smart, focused, and disciplined.

MAXIMIZE YOUR TIME

Tim Ferriss's book, *The 4-Hour Workweek*, is one of the dumbest I've ever read. Of course, you should try to be efficient and delegate well, as he advocates, but, especially early in your career, there's no substitute for hard work. Trust me, you are far more likely to get ahead if you are the first one in the office every morning and the last to leave.

I've never forgotten the line from a famous Hollywood executive, Peter Guber, who came to speak at Harvard

Business School while I was there. He said: "I've gotten ahead by working half days. And you know what? It doesn't matter which 12 hours a day I work!"

That's not hyperbole. Do the math: 12 hours a day dedicated toward your job/career/study/learning leaves 12 hours a day for everything else: eight hours of sleep, one hour of exercise, and three hours of eating, socializing, relaxing, etc. Then on weekends, cut your work in half to six hours—and be sure to take some wonderful vacations!

By the way, it's not just about putting in a lot of hours but also overcoming obstacles and having grit, determination, and resilience. We all face setbacks in life—it's how we handle them that's critical. One study measured students' IQ and grit and discovered that grit is twice as important in determining life outcomes. (The best research in this area is being done by Angela Duckworth, who wrote a book about it called *Grit: The Power of Passion and Perseverance*.)

GET EIGHT HOURS OF SLEEP

For most of my adult life, I felt guilty about getting anything more than six hours of sleep each night. I know a handful of people—like my friend Wendy Kopp, with whom I worked starting Teach for America in 1989-90—who perform at super high levels yet only sleep four hours a night.

How I envy them—I would pay a lot of money for a pill that allowed me to do this!

A few years ago, I tried to train myself to function on six hours of sleep, staying up until midnight and setting my alarm for six o'clock in the morning, but it didn't work—it just made me tired all the time, and I could tell my brain wasn't functioning 100%.

So I went back to my usual seven to seven and a half hours and felt guilty until last year when I saw a 19-minute TED Talk by Matt Walker called *Sleep Is Your Superpower*.

In it (and in his book that I subsequently read, *Why We Sleep: Unlocking the Power of Sleep and Dreams*), he shared the results of numerous studies, all of which show the importance of getting at least eight hours of sleep—and the terrible consequences of sleep deprivation. Premature aging ("the shorter your sleep, the shorter your life"). Early-onset dementia caused by Alzheimer's. Reduced ability to absorb, process, and remember things. Impotence. A suppressed immune system, resulting in higher cancer risk. Increased chances of auto accidents (like Susan's!), suicides, cardiovascular disease, and heart attacks.

Walker concluded:

"Sleep, unfortunately, is not an optional lifestyle luxury.

Sleep is a nonnegotiable biological necessity. It is your life-support system, and it is Mother Nature's best effort yet at immortality.

And the decimation of sleep throughout industrialized nations is having a catastrophic impact on our health, our wellness, even the safety and education of our children.

It's a silent sleep-loss epidemic, and it's quickly becoming one of the greatest public health challenges that we face in the twenty-first century."

Walker's wisdom changed my life. Instead of strategizing how to get *less* sleep, I now try to get *more*. Rather than viewing it as a wasteful luxury, I try to get a minimum of eight hours each night—and nine is even better!

While I am, of course, only a sample size of one, I can tell you that ever since I started getting more sleep, I feel more energetic and stronger, both physically and mentally.

(If you have trouble falling/staying asleep, there are many websites with lots of advice—and for serious cases, there's therapy, and I've found Ambien to be very effective, though I recommend avoiding this prescription drug if you can. Walker's tips include avoiding naps during the day and alcohol and caffeine in the evenings; going to bed and waking up at the same time every day, including weekends; and keeping the nighttime bedroom temperature at 65 degrees.)

REDUCE DISTRACTIONS

Spending a lot of hours in the office or library isn't worth much if you're constantly distracted, which is increasingly common.

I'll admit to being very prone to distractions. As a kid, I loved video games—even the primitive ones like *Space Invaders, Asteroids, Defender*, and *Donkey Kong*. I remember one year in high school when I memorized the patterns for every level of *Pac-Man* so I could play for hours for only a quarter—I shudder to think of how much time I wasted, sitting there alone like a zombie. After college, I binge-played *Risk* on the computers at Boston Consulting Group when I should have been doing work.

It's a constant struggle for me to rein in these distractions—and it's getting exponentially harder. Staying on track and focused is a bigger challenge today than at any time in history thanks to these three notorious time-killers:

SMARTPHONES & SOCIAL MEDIA

Our smartphones are the single-most pernicious distraction in society today. They beep and buzz constantly with updates, text messages, and email, making it a real challenge to get any work done. It even cost one woman I know of her job.

A business-owner friend of mine employs two dozen people to package and ship products from his warehouse in Dallas. One of these workers, a young woman in her twenties, was constantly checking her phone. Exasperated, my friend asked her to put it away.

"There's work to do," he said.

"Well," she replied, clearly annoyed, "I *do* have a personal life."

"Not on my clock, you don't," he said.

Ten minutes later, she pulled it out again.

My friend just pointed to the nearest exit and said, "There's the door. Get out. You're fired."

Smartphones are highly addictive, and I suspect this young woman is symbolic of a wider problem. Our brains have become used to the constant stimulation our smartphones give us, and we're now like rats in a science experiment, mindlessly checking our phones over and over throughout the day and getting little hits of dopamine every time to satisfy our craving.

BINGE-WATCHING

Not too long ago, there were only a dozen channels on TV, and you had to watch when a show aired or miss it forever. But today, streaming video services like Netflix and YouTube have not only killed rental chains like Blockbuster and impacted traditional television but also ushered in an era in which an unlimited amount of video entertainment is only a few swipes or clicks away. And it's not all schlock. In many ways, we're in a golden era of television, with thousands of hours of tremendously compelling content like *The Sopranos, The Wire, Breaking Bad, Friday Night Lights,* and *Game of Thrones* available at low cost.

It's so easy to get hooked on one or more of these shows (I speak from personal experience) and waste ungodly amounts of time!

VIDEO GAMES

Modern video games like *Fortnite, Minecraft, Red Dead Redemption, Grand Theft Auto,* and *Call of Duty* are wildly addictive, with their immersive plots and amazing graphics. Plus, you can play with friends (or strangers) all over the world. According to the Entertainment Software Association, more than 150 million Americans play video games (more than half of our adult population), wasting an average of six hours per week. 60% of Americans play video games daily.

I'm not one of them; ever since I broke my addiction to *Risk* at age 24, I've deliberately never played them because I know how addicted I became to the primitive games of my youth, so I can't imagine what would happen if I started playing these vastly superior games!

If you want to be successful, you need to make a conscious effort to reduce the distractions in your life.

ALWAYS MAKE A GREAT IMPRESSION

The most important factors that will determine your business and personal success are internal: are you smart, creative, hard-working, pleasant to be around, confident without being arrogant, completely reliable and trustworthy, etc.

That said, it's a highly competitive world, and many people have these characteristics, so first impressions and appearances matter.

Forgive me if some of this appears shallow—I'm not saying that this is how the world should be, but rather how it is. Why would someone trust you to take care of them—as a consultant, doctor, lawyer, money manager, etc.—if you don't take care of yourself?

FITNESS

In many professions—money management is a prime example—a lot of people are obsessed with fitness or are even former college athletes, so being fit helps make a great impression.

PERSONAL HYGIENE AND CLOTHING

Pay up for a good haircut. If your teeth are crooked, pay a good dentist or orthodontist to fix them. As for clothing, I'm a cheapskate value guy and grew up wearing mostly second-hand clothes, so it kills me to spend, say, $150 on a button-down shirt or pair of pants when I can buy similar items for $20 at Costco. I've come to realize, however, that having sharp-looking clothes for professional settings is a smart investment. It really does make a difference, both externally (making a great impression) and internally (I feel more confident).

If you don't know anything about clothing and style (I don't), then find a store you trust. As Buffett says, "If you don't know jewelry, know your jeweler." Ditto for clothes. I buy most of my clothes from two places, Costco (for casual, cheap clothes I wear at home, to the gym, etc.) and Rothmans, the largest independent men's clothing store in NYC (for nice clothes). My friend Jim Giddon is the third-generation owner of Rothmans so if you ever shop there, tell him you're a friend of mine, and he'll give you a nice discount.

BECOME A LEARNING MACHINE

Your brain is your single most valuable asset. It's not just what you know but how you process information and behave that will determine your trajectory in life.

Munger once said:

> "I constantly see people rise in life who are not the smartest, sometimes not even the most diligent, but they are learning machines. They go to bed every night a little wiser than they were when they got up, and boy, does that help, particularly when you have a long run ahead of you.
>
> Develop into a lifelong self-learner through voracious reading. Cultivate curiosity and strive to become a little wiser every day."

If you can reduce your distractions and carve out twelve focused hours a day for work/study/learning, you'll be well on your way to success, but how you use those hours is key. You must become a learning machine at work, at school, and in your personal life.

Starting in preschool, I've been incredibly fortunate to attend some of the best schools in the world: Bing Nursery at Stanford, Eaglebrook in seventh and eighth grade, Northfield Mount Hermon for high school, Harvard University for undergrad, and finally Harvard Business School.

After two decades of nonstop studying, I remember thinking when I graduated from HBS at the ripe-old age of 27, filled with the hubris Harvard seems to instill in many of its graduates, that I was ready to go forth and conquer, reaping the benefits of my hard work, prestigious degrees, and vast knowledge and capabilities.

How wrong I was!

In reality, I was an inexperienced naïf with nothing more than a good foundation for what I now know has been my lifelong learning journey.

To become truly successful, you must become a learning machine—get on a steep learning curve and never get off it. Every day for the rest of your life, you should strive not only to keep abreast of the major events of the world but also to learn something new.

WHAT DO YOU DO AWAY FROM WORK?

To become a high-performance learning machine, ask yourself some questions:

- **Am I keeping up with the world?** It's critical to develop the habit of reading one or more major newspapers every day like *The New York Times, The Washington Post, The Wall Street Journal,* and *The Financial Times* (I read all four).

- **Where in my life am I doing a deep dive?** It's important to develop a broad range of knowledge but equally important to go very deep in a few areas in which you become an expert. Such areas for me include investing, school reform, and, more recently, the coronavirus. To a lesser extent, I've also studied the Navy SEALs (including signing up for two grueling weekends with ex-SEALs), criminal justice reform, the opioid epidemic, political advocacy, all things related to Africa, and extreme sports/adventures.

- **Am I reading more than my social media feed?** If most of your reading is done on Facebook, Twitter, Instagram, and/or Snapchat, you're in trouble. True learning comes from reading in-depth articles and books by top journalists and authors.

AUDIBLE BOOKS

I used to read dozens of books a year, but as the number of emails soared to hundreds each day and I started reading more and more content on the web, the number of books I read slowed to a trickle. But then, a couple of years ago, I discovered Audible.com, and it's changed my life. Now, during every moment when I can't read—usually when I'm riding my bike, driving, working out at the gym, or walking somewhere—I put on Bluetooth headphones and, instead of cranking my favorite music, listen to a book, podcast or

YouTube. Even better, I've trained myself to listen at two- or even three-times speed.

In a typical day, I might go to the gym for 45 minutes and have a meeting or other event in Midtown, which is a 15-minute bike ride each way, so that's one and a quarter hours every day, which is equal to nearly four hours of a book at regular speed—a third of a typical 12-hour audiobook. Thus, I'm cranking through two books every week, which has enriched my life in innumerable ways.

THE IMPORTANCE OF GETTING TRAINING

If you're really smart and disciplined, you can make a lot of progress on your own, but to really master a subject area, profession, or other high-level skill, you're going to need training. In his book *The Talent Code*, Daniel Coyle argues that bringing true talent to light requires three ingredients: coaching, motivation, and practice.

Think about it: how does someone become a top-notch surgeon, musician, teacher, or pilot? In each case, they go to school to learn the basics and spend a minimum (as Malcolm Gladwell notes) of 10,000 hours practicing, but a key part of the learning is becoming an apprentice to one or more people who can teach the higher-level skills that they can't learn in the classroom.

It's true in athletics as well. Michael Jordan had personal drive and natural talent, but he became the greatest basketball player in history because he also had good coaches. Ditto for every other top athlete.

I started playing tennis when I was very young and eventually played high school varsity. But I wasn't good enough to play in college, so I ended up playing only a few times a year from roughly age 20 to 50. But then I started playing again with a group of friends in New York City and loved it, so I decided I wanted not only to get my old game back but also to raise it to the next level (or, in the parlance of the tennis rating system, go from a 4.0 to a 4.5).

Initially, I was playing once or twice a week with friends. I was having fun, but my game wasn't improving until I met a pro, Georgy Chukhleb, who's an excellent player (he'd probably be ranked in the top 1,000 players in the world) and instructor. I started doing one- to two-hour sessions with him every week, and he remade my backhand, taught me smart strategies, and had me hit thousands of balls in various focused drills to teach me new skills and hone my muscle memory. It has made a huge difference.

Similarly, no one becomes an expert investor on their own. The real ascension up the learning curve will only happen if someone with more experience teaches you. Legendary investor Julian Robertson of Tiger Management is a great example: so many of his protégés have launched successful, multibillion-dollar hedge funds that there's a name for them: "Tiger Cubs."

I should have taken the time to work for and learn from a veteran, but having rashly started my own fund without any of the requisite experience, at least I did the next best thing and got myself on a steep learning curve.

GET CREDENTIALED AND MOVE TO THE CITY

Scott Galloway, the serial entrepreneur and NYU Marketing Professor I mentioned earlier, has some great advice for young people: get credentialed and live in a major city.

An important part of becoming a learning machine is your environment. During your early years, this means, if you're lucky, attending a high-quality school where you'll be surrounded by smart students and teacher/professors from whom you can learn and earn one or more educational credentials (such as a bachelor's and, preferably, a graduate degree, ideally from a "brand name" school) that will open doors for you the rest of your career.

The second half of Galloway's advice isn't as obvious, but I think he's right that most folks, especially young people early in their careers, would be well served to live and work in a major city. You might think that with high-speed internet connections and more and more people working from home (accelerated, of course, by COVID), physical location would be less important, but I'd argue the opposite (again, especially for those early in their careers).

Major cities are where the action is—and, I think, will continue to be, even in a post-COVID world. We're in a knowledge-based world, and new companies, jobs, and wealth are being created at a rapid rate. To maximize your chances of a successful career (as opposed to merely a series of jobs), you want to be in the center of things to develop your skills and your networks.

Our oldest daughter, Alison, earned an Economics degree from Carleton, a fantastic small liberal arts college in Minnesota. During her job search in early 2018, as her graduation approached, she cast a wide net, but we encouraged her to come back to New York, a vibrant city that she knows well and where she, Susan, and I have strong networks. She did, taking a job as a consultant at Ernst & Young, where she's getting excellent training.

DEVELOP EXPERTISE

The world is too competitive these days to simply be a smart generalist. The best jobs (and highest incomes) are going to those who, yes, have a broad skillset but also develop deep expertise in a particular area.

I've never been able to find the exact quote, but I recall Munger at a long-ago WESCO annual meeting using a tennis analogy. In essence, he advised, "When you're young, you should practice your forehand, backhand, serve, overheads, and net game. But at some point, if you have a particularly great forehand, you should structure your life so that all you do is pound forehands all day long."

Deep expertise doesn't come from the general knowledge and skills you acquire in elementary school, high school, or college—that's just the foundation. You need to figure out what you're truly interested in and passionate about and then do three things: 1) get a job at a great firm with a strong training program; 2) get a graduate degree in your field from a prestigious institution; and 3) find multiple mentors for whom you can apprentice.

I was fortunate to get these things right in my twenties: I got a job at the Boston Consulting Group out of college, went to Harvard Business School, and worked with renowned HBS Professor Michael Porter for five years.

BUILD A FOUNDATION

Before you can start to develop specialized expertise, you need a solid foundation. Start by developing what Munger calls "a latticework of mental models," which is a fancy term for a broad background of knowledge in STEM, literature, psychology, one or more languages, etc., beginning as early as high school and continuing throughout the rest of your life. In part, you can do this by going to good schools and taking challenging courses, but it's critical to supplement your formal education with a lot of reading and traveling.

I regret that I didn't start taking an interest in investing until I was nearly 30 years old—very late—but at least when I did, I had a good foundation upon which to build.

I also didn't waste my time going down the rabbit holes of various other types of investing, like technical analysis. I quickly recognized that value investing was the most sensible approach and best suited my temperament, so I focused my efforts in that area, which helped me rapidly move up the learning curve. Before I knew it, I was teaching others.

DEVELOP THE "SOFT STUFF"

Your smarts, work ethic, and credentials are all important, but you need to marry them with what I call the "soft stuff" if you want to be a well-rounded, successful, happy person.

This is what Buffett once said to a group of students:

> "How I got here is pretty simple in my case. It is not IQ; I'm sure you will be glad to hear.

The big thing is rationality. I always look at IQ and talent as representing the horsepower of the motor, but that the output—the efficiency with which the motor works—depends on rationality. A lot of people start out with 400-horsepower motors but only get 100 horsepower of output. It's way better to have a 200-horsepower motor and get it all into output.

So why do smart people do things that interfere with getting the output they're entitled to? It gets into the habits and character and temperament, and behaving in a rational manner. Not getting in your own way.

As I have said, everybody here has the ability absolutely to do anything I do and much beyond. Some of you will, and some of you won't. For those who won't, it will be because you get in your own way, not because the world doesn't allow you."

BE NICE

This advice sounds so obvious, but I didn't follow it for most of my youth. I wasn't a bad kid, but I sure was full of myself. School came easily to me, so I looked down on other kids I didn't think were as smart. I was a terrible listener—but boy did I love to hear myself talk! I was much more interested in myself than I was in anyone else.

As a result, teachers liked me, but many of my classmates rightly viewed me as arrogant and obnoxious. I had a few close friends, but that was it. In my junior year of high school, my best friend Bob and I ran for class co-presidents. We looked great on paper: we were good students, knew the school well, and had a solid platform. But we lost to two classmates who were known for being potheads! Why? Simple: outside of a relatively small circle of friends, Bob and (especially) I weren't well-liked. A lot of students thought that we looked down on them—and, sadly, they were right!

Today I'd like to think I'm much less of a jerk than I was back then, thanks to a few things:

I got really lucky 30 years ago when I met and later married a wonderful woman who makes me a better person. I wish all of you similar good fortune in finding the right life partner—nothing will make a greater impact on your long-term happiness.

In addition, meeting so many extraordinary people in my life has humbled me.

Lastly, I read the classic book by Dale Carnegie, first published in 1936, *How to Win Friends and Influence People*. It's a corny title, I know, but it's sold more than 30 million copies. Its most important lessons can be summarized in this way: "Most people don't care very much about you. They mainly care about themselves. So if you want people to like you, show genuine interest in and appreciation for them."

This book was such a revelation to me! All those years, I thought people were as interested in me as I was in myself, but they weren't! I know it sounds crazy, but other people will like you more—and think you are more interesting—the *less* you talk about yourself and the *more* you ask questions about them. I'm not kidding. Try it and see! And then keep doing it for the rest of your life.

BECOME A GIVING MACHINE

My parents always told Dana and me (quoting from an email my mom sent me):

> "You have been born into the best time in world history and, mostly by accident of birth, have been given every opportunity—love, education, health, exposure to the world, and a decent living standard. If you take these gifts and use them to simply enrich yourself, then you—and we—will have failed. To be a success, you have an obligation to make the world a better place."

For me, becoming a giving machine has been a combination of big things—like full-time jobs, starting new nonprofit organizations, and serving on boards—and day-to-day little things like donating to dozens of charities and sending friends articles of interest, and remembering their birthdays.

Since I started becoming a more giving person about 25 years ago, my quality of life has improved dramatically.

Why? For starters, it makes me feel good. I also have many more close friends, and they forgive me when I screw up and do something that angers them (which I'm prone to doing more often than I'd like). When I ask a favor of someone, they're more likely to say yes. Every year, when I climb some scary mountains to raise money for KIPP, I hit up all of my friends, who donate generously.

WHY IT'S IN YOUR SELF-INTEREST TO BE A GIVER

The main reason I highly recommend being a giving person—helping others and making the world a better place—is that it's the right thing to do.

But what if you're naturally a selfish person—or just don't feel like you have the time or money to help others at this stage of your life? I would still argue that you should try to give more, purely out of self-interest, for the following reasons:

1. It'll give your life meaning and purpose, make you feel better about yourself, and lead to greater happiness.

2. It will help you both personally and professionally if others perceive you to be philanthropic; people will be more likely to trust and like you.

3. Charity boards and events are fabulous for networking and finding/cultivating mentors. Super-high-profile, busy people who would never take a meeting or even a call from you are happy to talk at the cocktail party of a charity event. This is especially true if they're the honoree or one of the chairs and you made a donation.

NICE GUYS FINISH FIRST

There's a myth that to get ahead, you have to be ruthless and nasty, and that nice guys are chumps who get taken advantage of. Nothing could be further from the truth. Over the years, I've been fortunate enough to meet some of the world's richest and most successful people: Warren Buffett, Charlie Munger, Bill Gates, Michael Bloomberg, Eli Broad, Jorge Paulo Lemann, Don and Doris Fisher, Reed Hastings, and over a dozen billionaires in the investment world. I never cease to be amazed at what genuinely nice and philanthropic people almost all of them are.

THE MYTH OF THE SUCCESSFUL LONER

Another myth out there is the individual success story—the guy who, solely through his own brilliance and hard work, rises to the top—someone like Bill Gates, Steve Jobs, or

Elon Musk. None of it is true. Nobody gets anywhere on their own. Every person who has achieved anything in life has done so by standing on the shoulders of others, usually starting with parents, then teachers, and other mentors.

ARROGANCE VS. HUMILITY

Having a lot of self-confidence, maybe even bordering on arrogance, can be a good thing. You're more likely to try bold things and not be deterred by setbacks. The key, however, is to marry this confidence with a healthy dose of humility, which will help you figure out the difference between trying something bold versus something that's just dumb, and whether to soldier on in the face of setbacks versus wisely pulling the plug on something that's never going to work.

Warren Buffett is a great example of someone who's struck the right balance. He has plenty of self-confidence—one of my favorite sayings of his is, "My idea of a group decision is looking in a mirror"—but he's also very humble. He's the world's most famous investor, but he's always saying he doesn't understand certain companies or industries, and he goes out of his way to talk about the terrible investments he's made over the years.

Ditto for Michael Porter. I met him 27 years ago at the end of my first year at Harvard Business School. He was (and still is) a big deal, the school's youngest tenured professor ever, the author of countless books, and an advisor to CEOs and government leaders around the world. If there's anyone who has good reason to be pompous and arrogant and do a lot of talking rather than listening, it's Michael Porter.

But when I worked with him for five years during and after business school, I observed the opposite. Sure, he had an ego, but he bent over backward to be kind to everyone he met, and he always listened to what they had to say with genuine interest. When he responded, he didn't put them down, even when he disagreed with what they were saying. I have tried to emulate him ever since.

MONEY DOESN'T EQUAL HAPPINESS

Professor Porter hired four other students and me to do research with him on how to revitalize the economies of inner cities. I did this for a year as a student, and then, as I was graduating, I turned down a cushy consulting job and signed on to be Executive Director of a nonprofit we created, the Initiative for a Competitive Inner City, which is still going strong to this day.

I did this for the next five years, and when I came back for my fifth reunion, I learned from a class survey that I had made less money since graduating than *every single one* of my more than 800 classmates. And you know what? I really didn't care. I loved my work and felt like our organization was making a difference. Susan and I weren't rich, but we earned enough to live comfortably and start a family. We were very happy.

I can tell you, both from personal experience and a lot of data, that once you're taken care of your basic needs, more money doesn't translate into more happiness. I know quite a few happy teachers and miserable billionaires. Seriously.

DEALING WITH MISTAKES

Everyone makes mistakes—they make a bad business decision, lose money, piss off a friend or family member, break something valuable, etc.

What differentiates people is how they handle it. It never ceases to amaze me how hard it is for so many people to admit a mistake, apologize, and, if possible, make up for it.

The proper response involves a five-step process:

1. What went wrong?
2. Why did it go wrong?
3. What parts of it were your fault?
4. Own it and learn from it (but don't obsess); and
5. Fix it. What can you do to make it right (or at least better)?

The hardest part is owning it. It's so much easier to distance yourself from a screw-up.

During one of my seminars, a student, when talking about a stock that went up a lot, said, "I bought Restoration Hardware." But later, when referring to a terrible stock that went to zero, he said, "We bought SunEdison."

I said, "Hold on a second. Who's 'we'? Did you get a partner that I haven't heard of?"

He sheepishly corrected himself: "I mean, *I* bought SunEdison..."

It was a small thing, but it spoke volumes—and we all do it.

If you can't own your mistakes, you'll never learn and never improve. You'll stumble through life, repeating the same mistakes over and over, a defective human being.

I had a little incident a while ago. I was backing my car into a tight spot and bumped the car parked behind me. When I finished parking, I was about to walk up the street to my apartment building when I saw a very large and intimidating guy with a lot of tattoos standing next to the car I had bumped. He said, "Hey, you hit my car!"

You can imagine the many ways this situation could have

gotten ugly. I was pretty nervous, so I said, "I'm really sorry. I didn't mean to. Was there any damage?" He replied, "You broke this," and pointed to a little plastic ornament attached to the front grill of his car. I could see that I'd broken it, but it probably could be glued back in place in about thirty seconds or replaced for a few dollars. Rather than argue the point, I said, "If I gave you $20, would we be good?" He smiled and said, "Sure!" Problem solved.

It's actually sometimes quite easy to admit you made a mistake, apologize, and make up for it.

But it doesn't come naturally to most people—my younger self included. I've gotten a lot better at it over the years. It's the right thing to do, and it makes big problems smaller—and little problems go away entirely. (By the way, if you can make a problem disappear by throwing an affordable amount of money at it, then it's not even really a problem!)

HOW TO APOLOGIZE

How many times have you seen someone do something really offensive and then make a mealy-mouthed I'm-sorry-if-anyone-was-offended apology? That just makes things worse!

There are five steps to any good apology:

1. Express remorse. Every apology needs to start with two magic words: "I'm sorry," or "I apologize." Don't say, "I'm sorry if you were offended."

2. Admit responsibility for what you did and how it harmed the person to whom you're apologizing.

3. Make amends. Is there anything you can do to fix it? If you're not sure, ask. Then do it.

4. Promise that it won't happen again.

5. Learn from it so that it really won't happen again.

CONCLUSION

A few years ago, I had the honor of giving the commencement address at my middle school alma mater, Eaglebrook School. As I was struggling to write a speech that would be both meaningful and memorable, my youngest daughter, Katharine, then 14, suggested, "Tell them about your Number One Immutable Law of the Universe," which is something I'd been saying to my daughters for years. Against the advice of some of my friends, I decided to share it with my audience in all of its unfiltered glory: "If you are a dumbass, there *will* be consequences!"

I like it because it's memorable. I'm pretty sure the word "dumbass" had never been used in any commencement address ever. The question is, was it meaningful? I think so. Let me use a sports analogy to explain why.

I love basketball. I've been playing pickup ball a few times a week for more than thirty years, and I've been an NBA fan ever since. Growing up in New England, I was crazy about Larry Bird and the Celtics. One thing I learned over all of these years is that while the scorers get all the acclaim, it's defense that wins championships—not just in basketball, but in pretty much every sport.

It's the same in life: the foundation of a successful life is playing defense—and by that, I mean avoiding the obvious mistakes that can really set you back.

Some of them are big, general things: if you make a mistake choosing a spouse or career, you're going to be miserable; if you're mean to people, don't expect to have many friends; if you're lazy and dishonest, people won't trust you, and you won't have much of a life; if you don't take care of your body, of course, it's going to break down. But I'm also talking about the blindingly obvious, easy things: always wear a seat belt and helmet; don't smoke, use drugs, or drink excessively.

It's also critical to understand that life isn't a steady upward march. Rather, it can be flat for long periods of time, in which you live in the same place, have the same job, earn roughly the same income, hang out with the same friends, and so forth. And then an opportunity comes along to take a huge leap forward, like getting into a top school or taking an incredible new job.

It may seem like these two periods are very different, but in fact, they're inextricably linked. During the flat periods, you might feel like you're in a rut, but you have to keep doing all the right things—expanding your mind, taking care of your body, working hard, building your relationships and reputation—because these things lead to the great opportunities that only come along periodically (sometimes, only once in a lifetime, like finding the right person to marry).

Instead of a steady upward climb, life is more like three steps forward, two steps back. Everyone focuses on those forward steps, but it's equally important to minimize the backward ones.

I hope this book has given you some food for thought on how to do this—and build a happy, successful life!

APPENDIX A

MY STORY

My parents were the third couple to meet and marry in the Peace Corps, tying the knot in a cathedral in Manila in the Philippines in December 1962, only a few months after meeting each other during training in Hawaii. My mom, the daughter of a Seattle fireman, had just finished college earlier that year at the University of Washington, while my father, from a prominent family in Connecticut (his grandfather was Majority Leader in the House of Representatives in the early 1900s), was still a year shy of earning his degree at Yale. It's the kind of marriage of people from vastly different backgrounds that you don't see much of anymore.

After finishing their two years in the Peace Corps in 1964, they moved to New Haven, where my dad finished college and earned a master's degree in education while they both worked as public school teachers. I came along in 1966 and

Dana in 1969. We were a tight family, but for the next dozen years, we were global nomads, never living anywhere for more than three years until I was a teenager.

First, we moved to Tanzania in 1968, where my dad developed a science curriculum and trained teachers at the Morogoro Teachers College for three years. I first attended school there—I was the only white kid in a class of local farmers' children, so I naturally wanted to be a farmer as well. My parents have pictures of me digging in our yard with a hoe. They tell me that I came home crying one day, saying that I wouldn't go back unless I could have black hair and black shoes like the other children. I didn't like being different, with my awful straight blond hair and ugly American sneakers.

We then moved to Palo Alto, CA, for three years, from 1971-1974, while my father started his Doctorate in Education at Stanford University. It was an idyllic time—like pretty much my entire childhood, come to think of it. We lived in Escondido Village, a huge graduate student housing complex where I had dozens of friends nearby.

I attended Bing Nursery School, where, when I was six years old, I was one of the roughly 600 children tested as part of the famous Stanford Marshmallow Experiment. We were presented with a single marshmallow and told if we didn't eat it, we would receive a second marshmallow at some point in the future. Researchers observed us through a one-way mirror to see if we had the self-control to wait.

They've been tracking us ever since, and the findings have been remarkable (though some are questioning their validity): the ones who exhibited self-control by waiting for a second marshmallow were far more likely to finish high school and college; scored an average of 200 points higher on the SAT; had lower rates of drug use, incarceration, and divorce; and earned a much higher annual income than those who didn't.

I'm often asked whether I ate the marshmallow. I don't know—they've never told any of us because it might bias our answers and ruin the experiment. But, based on my life outcomes, I assume I didn't...

In 1974 we moved to Managua, Nicaragua, where my father worked on a project that taught math to elementary school students across the country via radio. We were there for three years and got lucky on the timing, arriving soon after a devastating earthquake and leaving before the dictator, Somoza, was overthrown by the Sandinistas. Dana and I lived in a happy bubble, attending the American-Nicaraguan School and, sadly, learning very little Spanish.

I was a cocky little kid and totally hyperactive. Though never formally diagnosed, I'm sure I had ADHD. My third-grade teacher once pulled me out of the classroom and, in exasperation, pointed to the running track and said, "Just go run around for a while, and burn off some of that excess energy!"

We then returned to Stanford for a year—fifth grade for me—while my dad finished his doctorate.

My parents decided to settle down for Dana and my teenage years, so my dad took a job as the Academic Dean (dean of faculty) and my mom as Director of Student Activities at Northfield Mount Hermon School, a high school in western Massachusetts, two hours west of Boston on the Vermont/ New Hampshire/Massachusetts border. At the time, with 1,200 students, it was the largest private boarding school in the country.

I attended the local public elementary school for sixth grade, but then my parents scrimped and saved to send me to the elite, private Eaglebrook School in Deerfield, Massachusetts. The idea of having to travel 45 minutes each way every day to be a day student at an all-boys boarding school filled me with horror, but my parents ignored my screaming and crying, and off I went.

It was one of the most important of the many times they overruled me when I was too young and foolish to make the right decision myself. The difference between two years at Eaglebrook vs. the local junior high school I would have otherwise attended was night and day. It put me on a completely different educational trajectory that later helped me excel at Northfield Mount Hermon, which, in turn, propelled me to Harvard.

Of all the sacrifices my parents made for me, what they did to ensure I had a great education made the biggest difference in my life. It gave me a huge leg up though, to be honest, I didn't appreciate this until much later.

Because I had aced six Advanced Placement exams in high school, I had "sophomore standing" at Harvard and could have graduated in three years. I was in no rush, however, so I took some electives for half of my senior year and spent the other half as an intern at the US Embassy in Santiago, Chile, doing research for my senior thesis on "Reagan Administration Foreign Policy Toward Chile." I majored in government, with a specialty in international relations, and briefly considered a career in the foreign service, which would have aligned perfectly with my upbringing, but I was too interested in business.

This interest blossomed when I started working at Harvard Student Agencies, a student-run organization that provided students with employment and hands-on management opportunities. The summer after my freshman year, I sold advertising for the *Let's Go* series of travel guides along with

Bill Ackman, who remains a close friend and has become one of the world's best-known investors. We were both great salesmen and made more than $12,000 each, which at the time was a small fortune to us.

I had a good time at Harvard, but one of my great regrets is not taking full advantage of the educational opportunities there. It's a sink-or-swim environment: the undergraduate program isn't nurturing, and the classes are large. The school offers its students incredible resources, but it's up to them to make the most of what's available.

I don't feel like I did.

For example, Jeffrey Sachs, who's renowned for his work in the developing world, offered a class on the fight against global poverty. Given my interests and background growing up in Tanzania and Nicaragua, the class was right in my sweet spot, but because it was at 8 a.m. and I was too lazy to get up that early, I never took it. I look back on that decision with shame.

My parents tried to instill in me the value of being a learning machine, but I didn't fully embrace the concept until long after business school when I discovered Buffett and Munger. Until then, I was more of a shortcut machine—I sought ways to get the highest grades possible with the minimum amount of work all the way through college and business school, thereby missing countless opportunities to learn and grow along the way.

At one point during my undergraduate years, a friend invited me to sit in on a class at Harvard Business School. It was so riveting that I still remember the case to this day: a long-since bankrupt retailer, Consumers Distributing. I knew right then that I wanted to attend HBS.

But first, I had to get two to three years of work experience. I applied for jobs at all of the investment banking and consulting firms that recruited on campus and ended up getting offers from First Boston and the Boston Consulting Group.

But one day in the spring of my senior year, as I was weighing these offers, my friend David Kopp asked me, "Hey Whitney, what are you doing next year?"

I could tell by the way he asked that he had something in mind, so I replied, "Working at either First Boston or BCG. But what do you want me to do?"

He said, "My sister is graduating from Princeton and has an idea to build an organization like the Peace Corps for top graduating college students who would commit to two years of teaching in high-needs public schools in the US."

Frankly, I was skeptical, picturing a clueless do-gooder in

my mind, but I asked, "Who's your sister?" When he said, "Wendy Kopp," I slapped my forehead and said, "Holy cow! I know your sister!" The previous October, I had attended a conference in Washington, D.C., organized by a Princeton student group called The Foundation for Student Communication. The conference brought together CEOs of major corporations with student leaders from across the country. It was a really impressive, large-scale event, run entirely by students at an organization Wendy helmed.

So I got on the phone with her and immediately realized two things: 1) This was a big idea; and 2) If there was one graduating senior in the country who could pull this off, it was her, thanks to her Rolodex of CEOs plus incredible entrepreneurial, leadership, and management skills. So I deferred my job offer at BCG and signed up to help launch what became Teach for America.

To make a long story short, I was in over my head (the best that can be said is that I didn't sink TFA!), so after six months, I went back to Boston to start at BCG. I can't take any credit for what TFA has become, but I do take credit for recognizing a great idea and a brilliant entrepreneur.

I spent two years at BCG doing the standard two-year pre-business-school associate program. Frankly, I wasn't much of a consultant, but I learned some valuable skills. And, during my time there, I was lucky enough to meet my future wife. She was just starting Harvard Law School in September 1990 when Bill Ackman and I crashed the school's orientation booze cruise on Boston Harbor. Susan and Bill grew up in adjacent towns outside of New York City, so she recognized him and came over to chat. She's been unable to keep her hands off of me ever since (or at least that's my story, and I'm sticking with it!).

I was fortunate enough to gain acceptance to Harvard Business School and, after quitting BCG and backpacking around Africa for a few months, started there in the fall of 1992. I loved it!

In the spring of my first year, I joined a research project led by the school's most famous professor, Michael Porter, the guru of strategy and competitiveness. He was studying the economies of inner cities in the aftermath of the LA riots, trying to develop some new thinking on how to revitalize these distressed areas. After a year of work, he published an essay called *The Competitive Advantage of the Inner City*, which generated a great deal of interest and attention.

We wanted to continue the research and actually try to help minority-owned and inner-city-based businesses, so we created a new nonprofit called the Initiative for a Competitive Inner City (ICIC), of which Professor Porter was the part-time Chairman, and I became the full-time Executive Director upon my graduation in 1994.

It was a very exciting five years: we continued our pioneering research on the economic opportunities in inner cities, had teams of students from HBS (and, later, many more top business schools) do pro bono consulting projects for inner-city companies, and partnered with *Inc.* magazine on the annual "Inner City 100," in which we identified and celebrated the 100 fastest-growing inner-city companies in the country.

Meanwhile, after three years of dating, Susan and I were married in October 1993 during my second year of HBS. She had finished law school five months earlier and had taken a job at a law firm in New York City, so we had a commuter marriage for our first eight months until I graduated in May 1994 and joined her in NYC.

The next few years were hard on our new marriage because I was building and running an organization based in Boston, so I typically flew up on Tuesday mornings and returned on Thursday nights.

I loved my work, but three things led me to leave: 1) the ICIC had grown to the point where my job was less entrepreneurial and more managerial, which I hated; 2) our first child, Alison, was born in 1996, so I wanted to stop traveling so much (I still remember when I came home from a trip and Alison, seeing a loud, enthusiastic, strange man burst into the apartment, started crying; I didn't want to be that kind of distant father); and 3) I'd caught the investing bug and wanted to pursue that passion.

So, I left ICIC at the end of 1998 and launched what was surely one of the world's smallest hedge funds out of my bedroom on January 1, 1999, with $1 million from a handful of investors: myself, my parents and in-laws, and a few friends and family.

It was a reckless decision. I didn't consult with anyone, had no idea what starting a fund entailed, and had no investment strategy whatsoever. Investing is an apprenticeship business, yet I hadn't gotten the training, experience, and mentorship everyone should have before launching a fund. By all rights, I should have fallen on my face and failed.

But the opposite happened, at least for the first dozen years: I nearly tripled my investors' money in a flat market and grew assets to over $200 million.

Then, my lack of experience—and my success going to my head—caught up with me...I made a series of investment and business mistakes that led my fund to underperform the market over the subsequent seven years, which made me so miserable that I finally closed it in frustration in September 2017. (For the full story—it's a good one!—you'll have to read the other book I'm working on, *The Rise and Fall of Kase Capital.*)

Then, as I discussed earlier, I launched a new business, Kase Learning, teaching investing seminars. I loved the work but never figured out the marketing and struggled to get enough customers to make it a viable business. So, a little more than a year later, in early 2019, I partnered up with an old friend, Porter Stansberry, who founded and runs Stansberry Research, one of the largest investment newsletter publishers in the world. We jointly created Empire Financial Research, which publishes investment newsletters aimed at helping individuals invest wisely and profitably.

The business is going gangbusters, and I couldn't be happier. I get to do what I love—investing and writing—without the headaches of managing other people's money and with a team of folks at Stansberry Research handling legal, accounting, marketing, the website, customer service, etc.

EAGLEBROOK SCHOOL COMMENCEMENT ADDRESS

BY WHITNEY TILSON '82
FRIDAY, JUNE 3, 2016

Headmaster Chase, teachers, parents, friends, and fellow Brookies, thank you for inviting me back to Eaglebrook to speak to you. It is truly an honor.

I remember when I was sitting where you are 35 years ago, listening to the commencement speaker. She was delightful, but I have to confess that I don't remember anything she said.

So that's my challenge today: to say something that's both meaningful and memorable. That's a tall order.

I'd like to frame my remarks by telling you a little about myself and why I'm here. I don't think the school invited me to address you today because of my day job: I manage a hedge fund I started 17½ years ago. My business has been reasonably successful, but I'm not one of those billionaire hedge fund managers you read about.

No, I think I'm here because of what I've done in terms of making a difference in the world, in particular in the area of education reform.

My parents are both teachers—they met and married in the Peace Corps in 1962, and I grew up in Tanzania and Nicaragua—so I always had an interest in education, but my involvement really started when I was graduating from Harvard in 1989 and was weighing job offers from a few investment banks and consulting firms. But then a friend introduced me to his sister, who was graduating from Princeton, who had this crazy idea to recruit and train top graduating college students and send them into poor areas to teach for at least two years. His sister was Wendy Kopp, who was planning to start Teach for America. I thought it was a great idea and that she was a brilliant entrepreneur, so I deferred a job at the Boston Consulting Group and moved to New York City to help Wendy launch TFA that fall.

Being one of the early founders of something that's been so successful and impactful was a life-changing experience for me. It showed me that one person with a great idea and a lot of smarts and energy can have a huge impact on the world, and ever since, I've tried to follow in Wendy's huge footsteps.

Though I have a very full-time job, I make a big effort in my spare time fighting to make sure that every kid in this country gets an education that's even *half* as good as the one here. I won't bore you with the details, but I've been on the board of KIPP charter schools in New York City for more than a dozen years, helped start an organization called Democrats for Education Reform, and am a prolific writer and blogger on this topic. I'm motivated by a sense of outrage that this country has an educational system that is deeply unequal, in which poor and minority children, who most need the best schools and teachers, instead usually get the worst. I know that the education I've received has made all the difference in my life, and it really upsets me to know that millions of children in this country right now aren't getting a quality education and therefore have little hope of escaping the poverty that they were born into.

So with that, I'd like to talk to you about three things I've learned, based on my own experiences as a young man, being a father to three teenage daughters, and my involvement with education reform for the past 27 years.

The idea for the first one came from my youngest daughter, who just turned 14. I've done lots of public speaking, but I've never addressed an audience of young adults like yourselves, so I asked her what I should say. Her suggestion was: "Tell 'em about your #1 Immutable Law of the Universe," which is something I've been saying to my daughters for years. Against the advice of some of my friends, I decided to share it with you in all of its unfiltered glory, so here goes: "If you are a dumbass, there *will* be consequences!"

I like it because it's memorable: I'm pretty sure that the word "dumbass" has never been used in any commencement address ever. The question is, is it meaningful? I think it is. Let me explain why using a sports analogy.

Raise your hand if you like basketball—you play it or enjoy watching it? (I hear Eaglebrook had a good team this year.) I love the sport. I've been playing pickup basketball a few times a week for 30 years, and I've been an NBA fan ever since. Growing up here in New England, I was crazy about Larry Bird and the Celtics. One thing I've learned over all of these years is that while the scorers get all the acclaim, it's *defense* that wins championships—not just in basketball, but pretty much every sport.

It's the same in life: the foundation of a successful life is playing defense—and by that, I mean avoiding the obvious mistakes that can really set you back.

I'm not talking about the big, general things: if you're mean to people, don't expect to have many friends; if you're lazy and dishonest, you won't have much of a career; if you don't take care of your body, of course, it's going to break down...

No, I'm talking about the blindingly obvious things, ranging from touching a stove to see if it's hot (I did that once) or touching an electric fence to see if it's live (I did that too), all the way up to things that can derail—or end—a life.

Let me tell you about a young guy I know named Genarlow Wilson. Raised by a single mom, he grew up poor near Atlanta. Despite attending a number of tough schools, he was doing well in high school: he was an honor student, the star of the football team, homecoming king, and on his way to becoming the first person in his family to go to college. But then, during his senior year, he went to a party, got stoned and drunk, and, to make a very long and tragic story short, ended up in Georgia state prison for more than *two years*!

Believe it or not, I've actually been in jail—in Zimbabwe,

no less—for overstaying my visa. Talk about a boneheaded move! After I pled guilty, the judge banged his gavel and said, "I hereby sentence the defendant to 30 days in jail..." My heart was in my throat, and I thought I might faint! "Or," he continued, "a $10 fine." Guess which I chose?

But, look, I don't think any of you are going to end up in prison. That's not likely to be the thing that derails your life—so let me tell you what is. The biggie is alcohol.

Now that you're going off to high school and, only three years from now, college, you will soon be surrounded by very heavy drinking—one study showed that 44% of American college students had, in the previous *two weeks*, engaged in binge-drinking, defined as five or more drinks in a row. And these days, it's not beer—it's shots of hard alcohol.

You will likely face a lot of pressure to join in. My oldest daughter, a couple of years ago when she was a senior in high school, lost a lot of her friends, many going back to kindergarten because she didn't drink, so they didn't invite her to their parties. That hurt her a lot—but I'm really proud of her for not succumbing to peer pressure.

I'm not saying you should be a teetotaler—go ahead, have a drink or two...maybe even three. But be really careful about getting totally smashed because there are so many permanently bad things that can happen. Every week I read in the paper about teenagers dying in a car accident thanks to drinking (or, increasingly, texting) while driving. So maybe you're thinking, "I'll be safe—I'll just walk home from the party." Not so fast: really drunk people are far more likely to have terrible accidents like falling off a balcony or getting hit by a car walking home. Statistically speaking, you're *five times* more likely to die walking rather than driving a mile drunk. Lastly, if you drink frequently and heavily, there's a real risk of becoming an alcoholic. I have a relative who started drinking heavily in high school—and never stopped. It's ruined his life.

By now, you're probably thinking, "Jeez, what kind of commencement speaker is this? What a downer he is! When is he going to tell us how great we are, how we should put on our sunglasses because our future is so bright, and how we need to seize the day?"

Well, you are, and you should—but the reason I started with these stories is because the foundation for a successful life is playing good defense. If you want to get ahead, you have to start by not falling behind.

So now, let's turn to the fun stuff: playing offense and being successful in life. I have great news for you: the fact that you're graduating from Eaglebrook means that your odds of success in life are already off the charts. You've received a great education so far and will surely continue to. The vast majority of you have families who love and support you, and you have never known (nor will you ever know) violence, hunger, or homelessness—the kinds of things I saw up close growing up in Tanzania and Nicaragua, that I see when I visit my parents and sister, who live in Kenya today, and that I see every time I visit a school in an inner-city neighborhood in the US.

So congratulations: you are well on your way to winning the game of life...but you're still going to need to make a lot of good decisions and avoid a lot of bad ones along the way. I have plenty of experience with both, so I'd like to share two more pieces of advice.

But relax: I'm not going to lecture you! Instead, I'd like to tell you a few stories about my life and experiences that I hope will help you to achieve some of the success and happiness that I'm fortunate enough to have.

Before I do so, however, I want you to do some thinking. Look around at all of your classmates and ponder this question: who do you think is going to be really successful in life, not just financially, but in every way?

As you think about this, what are the characteristics you're focusing on? Is he smart? Does he work really hard and not give up easily? Does he have integrity? Is his word his bond? Is he 100% reliable? Is he well organized? Does he take care of himself and not take foolish risks? Is he a nice person and a pleasure to spend time with? Does he make the world a better place?

Now ask yourself: what is he doing that I can't do too? I think you'll find that at least 90% of these traits are things over which you have total control.

So you see, you don't need me to tell you what habits you should try to adopt—you already know. There's no secret— they're obvious! The real question is, what are you going to do about it?

The world's most famous investor, Warren Buffett, tells young people the following: "You can transform yourself into the person you want to be, but you have to decide early because the chains of habit are too light to be felt until they are too heavy to be broken."

Think about that. All the little things you do dozens of times every day—your habits—define who you are—and once these patterns are set, they're really tough to change.

So if you remember anything from today, I hope it will be this: it's critically important to develop good habits early in life.

I'm not going to spend any time today talking about obvious

good habits like eating healthily and exercising regularly, as important as they are. I'm only going to talk about two: work hard, be nice.

This is the motto of KIPP charter schools. As I mentioned earlier, I've been on the board of KIPP New York for more than a dozen years, but nationally it's a network of 183 schools in 20 states serving 70,000 students, 96% of whom are African-American or Latino and 88% of whom are poor. What KIPP is doing inspires me—for example, KIPP students are five times more likely to earn a four-year college degree than their peers.

On the walls of every KIPP school is the slogan, "Work hard, be nice!" [It's also the title of a great book about KIPP.] It's so simple that you might dismiss it, but if you think about it, those four words capture an awful lot of what you need to be successful in life.

Let's first talk about "work hard." You all are still a long ways from the working world, so for you, this is mostly about school. I can't stress enough how important it is for you to get into the habit of learning. Your single greatest asset is your mind, and how you develop it will largely determine how far you go.

Today, I consider myself a learning machine. I basically read nonstop, all day, every day. And not just about investing, which is my job—I try to read as broadly as possible. In my entire life, I have never met a single person who I consider to be well educated who doesn't read *a lot*.

You can start to become a learning machine today by downloading the app of a major newspaper like *The New York Times* onto your phone and start reading it every day. In addition, try to read a high-quality book every week or two, especially during the summer when you don't have as many demands on your time.

I'm embarrassed to admit that I wasn't always a learning machine: despite attending some of the best schools in the world—Eaglebrook, Northfield Mt. Hermon, Harvard, and Harvard Business School—most of the time, I cut as many corners as I could and, as a result, didn't learn nearly as much as I could have.

There were some exceptions, of course, when I was truly engaged in my learning. It started right here when I first discovered what an exceptional education really was. I had incredible teachers like Monie Chase and her class on the Revolutionary War. She got me so interested in the topic that I just dove in and learned everything I could about that time period. I especially remember the mock trial we had for Benedict Arnold, in which I was his defense attorney. What a learning experience—even though they still hanged my client!

Every one of you is going to attend a good high school and college. Don't waste this incredible opportunity by skating through like I did. For every class, even—or perhaps especially—the ones that aren't naturally the most interesting to you, dive in and learn as much as you can.

And never let up. It doesn't end with formal schooling. If you want to be successful in life, you need to be a *lifelong* learning machine, or everyone else will pass you by.

One last thought on "work hard": it's not just putting in a lot of hours, but also overcoming obstacles; having grit, determination, and resilience. All of us face setbacks in life—it's how we handle them that's critical. One study measured students' IQ and also grit—and it turns out that grit was twice as important in determining life outcomes. [The best research in this area is being done by Angela Duckworth, who's out with a new book about it: *Grit: The Power of Passion and Perseverance*.]

Okay, now let's talk about "be nice." Another way of saying this is: don't be a jerk!

I'm sure that sounds really simple, but it didn't characterize me for most of my youth. I wasn't a bad kid, but I sure was full of myself. School came easily to me, so I looked down on other kids who I didn't think were as smart. And I was a terrible listener—but boy did I love to hear myself talk! I was much more interested in myself than I was in anyone else.

As a result, teachers liked me plenty—but many of my classmates rightly viewed me as arrogant and obnoxious. I had a few close friends, but that was it. In my junior year of high school, my best friend Bob and I ran for class co-presidents. We looked great on paper: we were good students, knew the school well, and had a solid platform. But we lost to two classmates who were known for being *potheads*! Why? Simple: outside of a relatively small circle of friends, Bob and I weren't really well-liked. A lot of students thought that we looked down on them—and they were right!

Today I'd like to think that I'm much less of a jerk than I was back then, thanks to a few things:

- I got really lucky 26 years ago when I met and later married a wonderful woman who makes me a better person. I wish all of you similar good fortune in finding the right life partner—nothing will make a greater impact on your long-term happiness;
- I've met so many extraordinary people in my life that I no longer view myself as so extraordinary—it's humbled me; and
- Lastly, I read the classic old book, first published in 1936, *How to Win Friends and Influence People*. It's a corny title, I know, but it's sold more than 30 million

copies. Its most important lessons can be summarized in three sentences: Most people don't care very much about you. They mainly care about themselves. So if you want people to like you, show *genuine* interest in and appreciation for them.

This book was such a revelation to me! All those years, and I thought people were as interested in me as I was in myself—but they weren't! I know it sounds crazy, but other people will not only like you more, but they will think you are more interesting the *less* you talk about yourself and the *more* you ask them about themselves. I'm not kidding—try it, and you'll see! And then keep doing it for the rest of your life.

Another part of not being a jerk is being grateful. I really hope you are aware of—and grateful every day for—what you have. My best friend's wife works at a KIPP school in the toughest, poorest neighborhood of Philadelphia, and the stories she tells me break my heart: students your age who can barely read. And just this week, she told me about one student, a good kid, whose mother kicked him out of their home, and he now has a choice: be homeless or go live with his dad, who beats him.

At least these children are lucky enough to attend a KIPP school, which gives them a fighting chance in life. But they're the lucky few: the vast majority of kids like these attend dilapidated, underfunded, overcrowded schools in which little if any learning is going on.

The last thing I'd like to talk about, also related to "be nice," is being a giving person.

My parents always told my sister and me (and this is from an email my mom sent me this week): "You have been born into the best time in world history and, mostly by accident of birth, have been given every opportunity—love, education, health, exposure to the world, and a decent living standard. If you take these gifts and use them to simply enrich yourself, then you—and we—will have failed. To be a success, you have an obligation to make the world a better place."

I know it's a cliché, but as the saying goes, "If it's trite, it's right!" And there was an important added bonus: I discovered that the more I gave, the more I got back in return.

For me, giving back—becoming a giving machine—has been a combination of big things like full-time jobs, starting new nonprofit organizations, and serving on boards like KIPP, which I've already talked about, but it's also lots of day-to-day little things.

There are so many examples I could give, but here's one I do every day: if I find a mess, I clean it up—yes, even if I didn't make it. My pet peeve these days is my daughters leaving their dirty dishes in the sink.

Trust me, if you go through life leaving messes for other people to clean up (like I used to), they're going to resent you. In contrast, if you not only clean up after yourself but others; if you do more than your fair share, offer the other person the bigger piece of dessert, remember their birthday, give them an unexpected gift, it will make such a difference.

Since I started becoming a much more giving person about 20 years ago, the quality of my life has improved exponentially.

Why? For starters, it makes me feel good. I also have many more close friends—and they forgive me and stay my friends even when I screw up and do something that makes them mad at me (which I'm prone to doing more often than I'd like). When I ask a favor of someone, they're more likely to say yes. A month from now, I'm climbing two famous peaks in Europe—Mont Blanc and the Matterhorn—to raise money for KIPP, so I've been hitting up all of my friends—and they've already donated nearly $100,000. Lastly, while this may sound crass, having a well-deserved reputation as a good guy really helps my business. Other investors are more inclined to share investment ideas with me, and my investors are more likely to stay in my fund rather than yanking their money when my performance stinks, as it has over the past year.

To repeat what I said earlier: the more I give, the more I get back—and it leads to an immeasurably happier life.

I've thrown a lot at you here, so let me quickly summarize: defense wins championships, work hard, and be nice.

If you do these things, I promise you that you'll lead a long and rewarding life filled with love, laughter, and happiness.

It's yours for the taking.

Thank you, and congratulations to the class of 2016!

ACKNOWLEDGMENTS

Thank you, mom and dad, for being such amazing, loving parents and teaching me so many important life lessons.

Thank you, Warren Buffett and Charlie Munger, for putting a framework around what my parents instilled in me.

And thank you, Susan, for your boundless love and patience!

ABOUT THE AUTHOR

WHITNEY TILSON has always prioritized avoiding calamities in both his personal life and in his career. He graduated with high honors from both Harvard College and Harvard Business School, has had a successful career building multiple for-profit and nonprofit businesses, is happily married after 27 years, and has three wonderful daughters. Despite riding his bike in the streets of Manhattan every day and being an accomplished obstacle course racer and mountain climber, he's never had a serious accident. Whitney is passionate about sharing what he's learned with others through this book as well as the many newsletters he publishes at his firm, Empire Financial Research.

9 781544 520322